Anonymous

Special Report

to the governor of Louisiana on the mouth of Red river and the falls at

Alexandria, January 23, 1874

Anonymous

Special Report
to the governor of Louisiana on the mouth of Red river and the falls at Alexandria, January 23, 1874

ISBN/EAN: 9783337373580

Printed in Europe, USA, Canada, Australia, Japan

Cover: Foto ©Suzi / pixelio.de

More available books at **www.hansebooks.com**

SPECIAL REPORT

OF THE

Board of State Engineers,

TO THE

GOVERNOR OF LOUISIANA,

ON THE

MOUTH OF RED RIVER AND THE FALLS AT ALEXANDRIA.

JANUARY 23, 1874.

NEW ORLEANS:
PRINTED AT THE REPUBLICAN OFFICE, 94 CAMP STREET.
1874.

REPORT.

OFFICE OF THE BOARD OF STATE ENGINEERS.
New Orleans, January 23, 1874.

To His Excellency W. Pitt Kellogg, Governor of Louisiana:

GOVERNOR—In answer to the petition of many citizens in regard to the removal of the obstructions to navigation existing in Red River, at the falls at Alexandria, and in Old River, near its mouth, which was referred by your Excellency to the State Engineers, we would most respectfully make the following reply:

As we have neither the time nor means at our disposal to make a proper survey, for a full and special report of the condition of these obstructions in time for legislative action at this session, we have availed ourselves of the knowledge before us, and herewith present an array of facts that will demonstrate the importance of removing these obstructions, and without entering into a detail of the plans that have been proposed to accomplish these objects, will give some general ideas of them.

One of the Assistant State Engineers, Colonel E. H. Angamar, having been familiar with these subjects for many years, was assigned to prepare a paper on the subject of the closing of the mouth of Old River, and there will be found herewith his report, with a very interesting series of maps and plans, exhibiting the changes that have occurred, about " Old River " since A. D. 1578, and also his proposed plan to restore the Mississippi, the Red and Atchafalaya to the corelative positions they occupied at that distant date—three hundred years ago. It will be seen by reference to plate No. 3, of the accompanying maps, that his proposition is to build a series of dams or dikes across Old River at suitable points, and then dig canals for the Red River to enter the Mississippi far enough above the head of the Atchafalaya (as it will then be) so that there may be space sufficiently great to let the current of the Mississippi carry away the sediment, that would otherwise be deposited in Old River.

Colonel Angamar has not presented an estimate of the cost of the works he proposes, but in the extracts from the reports of former State

Engineers, which will be found herewith, an idea can be formed of the magnitude of the work. So many surveys have been made and the matter so thoroughly discussed in former times, by eminent engineers, that we have thought that on account of the importance of the subject it would be very proper to make copious extracts from some of the reports, that those who have an interest in the matter can form intelligent opinions as to the best mode of overcoming these obstructions, and especially also that these important measurements and suggestions may be condensed and perpetuated, as there are but few copies of these reports now in existence, and our present generation of reading men should have the benefit of them.

By a reference to plate 9, the localities mentioned can be understood.

There was a proposition to turn Red River through Bayou Cutoff, between Blackhawk and Union Point, but it was found that the Mississippi at low water was above the low water in the Red River.

Another plan was to close the Atchafalaya at Simmsport, and let all the Red River come down the Mississippi to the Latenach, where an outlet was to be made.

Several other plans will be found in the extracts we give, all of which are very costly; but by far the cheapest and simplest *experimental* plan which we would propose, is to build a low water dam from Turnbull's Island to the main land, between the mouth of the Red and head of the Atchafalaya, and force low water above Turnbull's Island. Our reasons for this plan are short: The lower mouth of Old River is now open in the lowest water (see extract from Commission of Engineers of 1874), and even when the Mississippi was six feet above low water, the current was running out of both mouths in August, 1873. Should this dam be but a few feet above low water, say two feet, the pressure against it would only be the fall of the water around Turnbull's Island at any stage of water, and the tumble, when the water would run over it, would only have this fall, say twenty inches, which always being on a water cushion, would do no damage. This would force all the water in low water above the island, and when the junction at the lower end of the island is reached, it would be more apt to pass out a larger portion to the Mississippi than now by the short and direct line at the head of the island. This might possibly injure the low water navigation of the Atchafalaya: but, as that country will soon be reached by railroads, a few weeks of low water will affect it but little, for, of course, this experimental plan will not affect the high water navigation; for, if the Atchafalaya is left as an outlet, the Mississippi will always scour out a channel when it rises over its *falling water* deposit.

A dam of the kind that we would propose would cost but a very small amount, for it would simply be the rough framed timber coffer dam that is used to close small crevasses, and, as we demonstrate, the pressure could not be more than twenty inches of water, unless the lower mouth of Old River should close again, and leave the Atchafalaya dry, when it would have to resist full low water depth ; but, as this is not probable, it is evident that light timbers could be used.

In regard to the falls at Alexandria, we must make the same remark as at first, that we have not been able to make a survey, and therefore must fall back upon the reports of our predecessors ; we regret to say that some of the most accurate and important reports on the falls are not to be obtained, as they too and nearly all the maps were destroyed at the burning of the capitol at Baton Rouge, but those that we have been able to collect we give herewith for the same reasons before mentioned.

Many surveys and reports have been made, and the engineers have differed as to the following manner of overcoming this obstruction. It has been proposed to build locks and dig a canal around the falls.

To open and enlarge the Bayou Rapides.

To remove the falls.

Or cut a deep channel through the rocks.

To contract the water-way by jetties, and create a deep, swift channel.

Each of these plans has had its champions, some as the best and some as the cheapest, but the only one completely tried was the jetties, which General Bailey built to pass out the Federal fleet in 1863. His plan is certainly the cheapest, but its permanency is questionable, even when well built.

We can suggest no experiment at the falls that could possibly come within the power of the State in its present financial condition, and therefore, leaving the reports and extract as food for reflection for all interested, we must only suggest that it can be demonstrated that both the overcoming of the obstruction to navigation at the falls and at the mouth of Red River are truly national works, and that the General Assembly of Louisiana now in session should at once memorialize the Congress of the United States on the subject, and ask that the falls of Red River should be treated as the falls of the Ohio, the Mississippi and other falls, and the mouth of Red River be kept open as the mouth of the Mississippi, and that surveys be made of these localities (unless those now on file in the office of the Chief of Engineers be sufficient) having these purposes in view.

Should the General Assembly fail to memorialize Congress, or should Congress fail to direct the surveys and reports to be made, your Excellency's order to the State Engineers will insure a complete survey and estimate before the next assembling of the Legislature of this State.

I have the honor to be, your obedient servant,

M. JEFF. THOMPSON,
Chief State Engineer.

NEW ORLEANS, October 14, 1873.

To His Excellency, W. P. Kellogg, Governor of Louisiana :

SIR —The undersigned respectfully beg leave to call the attention of your Excellency to the fact that the commerce of the Red River valley is gradually but steadily being diverted from this, its natural market, and transferred to St. Louis, Louisville and Cincinnati.

It is the opinion of a majority of our people that the only way to restore and secure to this Commonwealth the trade of that extensive and fertile section of country is to improve the navigation of Red River, and thereby reduce the cost of transportation on the same to such a low rate that competition from the distant West will be rendered impossible. The Federal Government having assumed the removal of the Big Raft, the two principal points now requiring attention are the "Falls at Alexandria" and the "Old River," which has of late filled up to such an extent that it is apprehended that unless something be done soon all water connection between the Red, Ouachita and Atchafalaya Rivers with the Mississippi will be at an end.

Therefore we pray that you direct the board of State Engineers to examine into the premises and report what measures would be required to prevent said result, the effect of which would be so disasterous to the prosperity of the State of Louisiana and the city of New Orleans in particular.

Very Respectfully,

McGehee, Snowden & Violet, 191 Gravier.
John T. Hall, 191 Gravier,
J. W. Burbridge, 190 Gravier.
Lehman, Abrams & Co., 184 and 186 Gravier,
John Phelps & Co., 192 Gravier,
Meyer, Weis & Co., 194 Gravier,
J. E. Carlin, 5 Delta,
Jurey & Gillis, 194 Gravier,
T. & S. Henderson, 38 Perdido,
John M. Sandidge & Co., 39 Perdido,
Alcus, Sherck & Autey, 36 Perdido,
Lord & McPeake, 70 Gravier,
C. L. Walmsley & Co., 31 Perdido,
John T. Hardie & Co., 67 Carondelet,
David Hadden & Co., 67 Carondelet,
W. J. Frierson & Co., 77 Carondelet,
T. L. Airey & Co., 71 Carondelet,
Perkins, Swenson & Co., 64 Carondelet.
Samuel Barrett, 62 Carondelet.
Aiken & Watts, 60 Carondelet.
John Chaffe, Bro. & Son, 55 Union.
Clappe, Bros. & Co., 50 Union.
Stewart, Bros. & Co., 46 Union.
Rawlings & Murrell, 45 Union.
Block & Brittin, 48 and 50 Canal.
George D. Hite, 4 Tchoupitoulas.
Nalle & Cammack, 193 Gravier.
G. W. Sentell & Co., 195 Gravier.
C. C. Peckett, master steamer Trenton.
B. R. Splane, pilot steamer Lessie Taylor.
H. A. Dunbar, pilot steamer S. B. Trenton.
S. H. Patterson, steamer Stella Black.
J. C. Mitchell, N. O. G. E. packet Co.
Chas. Thorn, steamer Carrie A. Thorn.
W. J. Boardman, steamer John T. Moore.

H. L. Lee, steamer Gladiola.

M. Wood, steamer La Belle.

Gus. Hodge, steamer Bastrop.

J. W. Blanke, steamer Lotawana.

L. P. Delahoussaye, steamer Bastrop.

H. H. Broad, steamer Bertha.

James A. Aiken, steamer C. H. Durfee.

REPORT OF E. H. ANGAMAR, Assistant State Engineer.

New Orleans, January 12, 1874.

To the Honorable Board of State Engineers:

Agreeably to a resolution of this Honorable Board, that I should prepare a report on that part of a petition of sundry influential citizens of this State to the Governor, wherein they "pray that this board should examine into and suggest what measures would be required to prevent the filling up of Red River and the threatening separation of the Mississippi from the Red and Atchafalaya rivers." I beg leave to respectfully submit the following, to wit:

Old river (that part of the old channel of the Mississippi river surrounding the Island formed by the Shreve Cut-off) is about seventeen miles long. About six miles from its head is the mouth of the Red River, and two miles further is the head of the Atchafalaya the lower part of said Old river having been closed many years ago, the upper part is the only navigable link of communication, through which can be brought to New Orleans, their natural market, the immense products of that most extensive and fertile territory composed of the Ouachita, Tensas, Red River, Atchafalaya and Opelousas valleys, besides those of a large portion of Northeastern Texas and Southeastern Arkansas, (the lower part of Old river has lately reopened itself and steamboats are now using it, but it is an accidental and momentary opening only bound to gorge up and close again shortly, and will not be considered in this report). From an official report of the committee on Internal Improvements of the General Assembly, of this State, of 1871, we see that "the yearly shipments of cotton from that section of country amount to 300,000 bales, which, with other products and return supplies, swell its commerce to 100,000 tons, worth about $50,000,000, requiring for its transportation a steamboat tonnage of about 10,000 tons, and giving rise to mercantile operations of about $100,000,000 per annum."

The above official quotation requires no comment to demonstrate how deeply important it is to the State of Louisiana and the City of New Orleans to secure that commerce and prevent its diversion; and the uneasiness of our people as to its threatening loss can be easily appreciated when we state that the stream over which must be transported the immense amount of products above specified ("Old River"), which formerly was about a mile wide, is now hardly 400 feet wide in many places, and that the channel, once about eighty feet deep, is now hardly four feet deep at low water, and has been as shallow as twenty-seven inches. (See the undersigned's Report to the General Assembly of 1860.) In fact, that navigation would have been destroyed long since were it not for the temporary reliefs applied to it at different times, by appropriations of money, by the work of State boats, and by means of cut-offs, at a total expenditure amounting to no less than one million dollars.

In 1845-46-47, the navigation of Old River was so very near being entirely suspended that the then Board of Public Works proposed and executed the "Raccourci cut-off."

Governor P. O. Hebert, then State Engineer, opposed that measure very strenuously, and stated at the time that the relief so afforded to that navigation would have a temporary effect only, and that, within a few years the Mississippi would resume its old level and fill up again the gorges of the Old River. (State Engineer's Reports 1846-47.[*])

The predictions of the far-seeing engineer have unfortunately been realized, and the prospects of losing all navigable communication between the Red and the Mississippi rivers are now just as threatening as they were before the above temporary reliefs were applied, and it is the opinion of all practical men, engineers, captains and pilots, that the longer we wait before taking action in the matter, the greater will be the difficulty and greater also will be the cost.

In fact it is a prevailing opinion, based upon facts, that were it not for the large and yawning crevasses left open since the war in the upper river parishes, and through which an immense volume of Mississippi water is poured into Red and Ouachita Rivers, and which more than doubles their natural water discharged, the "Old River" channel would have been before this day among the things of the past.

The danger and the necessity of action in the premises being

---

* Extract from the Engineer's Report, 1847: "Bien que je ne puisse m'empêcher de reconnaître les dangers dont la navigation de la Rivière Rouge est menacée par suite du Shreveport cut off, cependant je n'ai aucune raison de changer mon opinion relativement au cut off de l'anse du Raccourci cut off. Ce cut off ne peut pas améliorer la navigation de la Rivière Rouge d'une manière permanente et ferait certainement beaucoup de mal à la partie inférieure de l'État."

once admitted, now comes the practical question, "How can the threatening danger be prevented, and how can that all important navigable communication between the Red and Mississippi rivers be secured in a permanent manner?"

For the eighth time does this matter now come before our Legislature: 1846, 1847, 1855, 1856, 1859, 1860, and 1861, when the writer of these lines was called upon to submit to the Legislative Assembly a report upon the subject, and, in answer to the above question will say, let us first inquire into the causes by the workings of which the results or effects to be overcome have been produced, and then it will be much easier to find out the remedy for it.

In this case, the cause of the disorder is so very plain that our task will be quite easy. It will suffice to examine and compare the series of maps of Old River in our possession ; they are a true, almost tangible history of the case, and will point out to us, in a most forcible manner by what agencies the present state of things has been brought about, and how they can be counteracted and overcome.

The first map we submit (plate No. 1) is a copy of a map dated 1578, nearly three hundred years ago! drawn by a monk named Ptolemy, a Venitian, who was a member of the De Soto party, the first white men who ever floated on the bosom of Red River. (The original is deposited in the National Library of Madrid, Spain.)

The next map of record of the same locality bears date of 1722 (about one hundred and fifty years later) ; it was drawn by a French engineer named Broutin; its outlines are so similar to those of the map of the Monk Ptolemy that we did not think necessary to reproduce it. The only noticable difference between the two being that in the map of Broutin there is marked a double line with the accompanying words : "Portage de la Croix" (Portage of the Cross), which does not exist in the Ptolemy map, and extends from bank to bank across the short neck of land where the distance from river to river is the shortest, and where about one hundred years later the Shreve cut-off was executed.

That portage must have been a military corduroy road opened by the French to facilitate transportation of military stores to Fort Tunica, at that time garrisoned by troops of that nation. (The original of that map is at the Grand Library of Paris, France).

The third map of record (also included in our plate No. 1) is by

a French engineer named Lafon, who was a member of the famous
Bienville expedition. It is dated 1805 ; its outlines correspond
exactly with the other two ; the only peculiarity about it being that
it is the first map where the Atchafalaya is put down by its real
name ; that stream being designated in the maps of Ptolemy and
Broutin without any name of its own, and only by the words,
" Riviere qui va au Grand Lac des Schetimaches" (river leading to
the Grand Lake of the Schetimaches). (The original of said map
can be seen at the Grand Library of Paris.

The fourth map of record, and also included in our plate No. 1, is
by the State engineer : it is dated 1830—and offers no peculiarities
other than its perfect resemblance with the others (the original
was in the State library in the capitol at Baton Rouge, and was there
destroyed by fire). The four maps above mentioned, and all com-
prised in our plate No. 1, cover a period of more than two hundred
and fifty years ; their outlines are so much alike that any one of
the four can answer for the others, and they demonstrate to us in
an undeniable manner, that before the hand of man interferred with
the laws of nature, and the regimen of the Mississippi by the fell-
ing of forests, the building of levees, the digging of cut-offs, and the
washing of the banks by steamboat waves, the meanderings of
the big river were not of a changeable nature as they now are, and
the caving of the banks, now so frequent, were almost unheard of ;
these maps show us that, during that very long period of time; the
course, width and shape (and of course the depth) of the Mississippi around the bend now known as " Old River" remained
unchanged.

In those maps we see that during the two hundred and fifty years the
Mississippi has been plowing his mighty waters around Old River;
that about midway down in the bend the *Tributary* (Red River)
was *emptying* its waters *directly* into the main river and that, a little
below, the *outlet* (Atchafalaya) was receiving its waters *directly* from
the main river.

In 1830, a man named Shreve (the founder of Shreveport), who
was keeping a ferry boat at the foot of the bend where was "the
portage of the cross," undertook to cut a ditch across that narrow-
neck of land and exactly where the "portage road" was.

The poor, uneducated man had no idea, probably, that the digging of this little ditch would eventually be the making of a new

Mississippi river. However, at the next flood, the Mississippi finding as much fall (2 feet 6 inches,) within the distance of a few hundred yards as it formerly had around a bend of seventeen miles, went at once jumping, roaring and tearing through the new channel and in a few months time cut out for itself a full size bed sufficient to accomodate its waters; and thus the insignificant ditch of the unsuspecting ferryman soon became a big river capable of bearing on its wide bosom thousands of steamboats laden with the products of this immense continent.

During that eventful year (1830–1831), immediately after the opening of the cut-off, no very perceptible changes occurred in Old River, besides the slacking up of the current and its almost lake-like appearance (see in plate 2 the lines thus marked — - - — - -) but from that date out changes, great and rapid, and well defined, have made their appearance. Look at the same plate 2 dated 1839, eight years only after the cut-off, and follow the outlines thus marked - - - - - - - and we will see that the upper part of Old River has become greatly contracted, especially near the head, and that its lower end, near the Mississippi, has been filled up to such an extent that the separation between the two streams is almost complete. Those lines are from a map by the late talented Louis Bringer, who for many years held the responsible position of United States Surveyor General in the State; (the original was deposited in the State Library at Baton Rouge and was destroyed by fire during the late war). The outlines indicated in the same plate No. 2 show the changes that had occurred within the sixteen years following the opening of the cut-off; they are from a map by that sterling engineer, the late D. A. Randall, who had general charge of the State snag boats for many years, and cleared more bayous and done more work of improvements on our navigable streams than any other man. Said map is dated 1847, and shows the continuation of the same process of filling up already apparent in the preceding, with this difference only that the results are much more forcibly delineated. Upper Old River is still more contracted, and is taking a more southerly coarse near the place of meeting with the Mississippi, and lower Old River does not communicate any more with the Missis- sippi. It was at that time that the complete separation of the two rivers became so threatening that, as we have stated above, the momentary relief of the Racconrci cut-off was resorted to.

Plate No. 2. indicates also the outlines of an original map, dated 1859, and since destroyed by the fire of the State House at Baton Rouge, drawn by the writer of the report after a most careful survey and soundings.

It shows that notwithstanding the relief afforded by the Racconrci cut-off, the laws of nature whereby the separation of the Red from the Mississippi River was being operated, have resumed the ascendency and continue their slow but unremitting and sure work: upper Old River has become a narrow, contracted and shallow stream, with only twenty-seven inches of water over the bar in the month of September. When said map was drawn, a period of thirty-five years only had elapsed since the Shreve cut-off, and during that time the work of filling up executed by the Mississippi in Old river had amounted to the figure of 5,750,000,000 cubic yards of earth, which at the rate of cost paid this day for moving earth, would amount to the appaling sum of $2,887,500,000 or $825,142,800 per year! What a pity our poor taxpayers can not turn the energies of such a terrible worker as old Meschacébé to building up the levees. In order to judge of the amount of filling up done during that period look at profile plate 6. Plate 5. is a theoretical and imaginary map, drawn by the undersigned, indicating what will be the ultimate result of the laws of nature that have worked the state of things exhibited in plates Nos. 2, and 3, unless some artificial means are resorted to for the purpose of preventing the separation of the two rivers.

It is not insisted upon that the realization of this imaginary map will take place this or next year, nor as long as the large crevasses in the upper river parishes are left open; but that, under the existing influences, it will happen sooner or later is a matter of undoubted certainty.

Now let us resume and draw from what precedes such conclusions as the maps we have submitted will lead us to.

From plate No. 1 covering a lapse of time of about two hundred and fifty years, we have seen that formerly the three rivers, Mississippi, Red and Atchafalaya were in direct communication in the bend now called "Old River;" the tributary (Red River) then emptied its waters directly into the main river, and the outlet (Atchafalaya) received its waters directly from the main river, and as long as said rivers remained in that relative position, no tangible changes in their course, size and shape could be seen.

Plate No. 11 has shown us that in 1830, the Shreve cut-off was effected, whereby the main river ceased to send the bulk of its waters through the old river bend and taking the short and more inclined shute offered by the cut-off, abandoned, as it were, its wonted channel and consequently ceased to be in the same immediate and direct connection with the two smaller streams; and that, from that day, the bed around the old bend commenced filling up in a steady and continuous manner ; and hence we plainly see and are compelled to acknowledge that the change in the correlative position of the three rivers occasioned by the Shreve cut-off is the cause of the disorders that have followed ; and hence also we are brought to the very forcible conclusion that, in order to put an end to said disorders and their detrimental consequences, we must try and replace said three rivers in their original correlative positions, knowing that the cause of the disorder being once removed, the disorder itself will be bound to disappear and matters will reassume their normal and natural state.

From the above we have ascertained that the cause of the filling up of Old river is the disruption or the separation of that part of the river from the main river, and it follows that to prevent its complete filling and the loss of all water communication now threatening we must replace said rivers in the same direct communication they were in during the period extending from 1578 to 1830.

And now comes this important question, how can it be done ? To which we will very readily answer by referring the reader to Plate No. 4, (another conjectural map of ours), where he will see that, and how we have replaced the three rivers (the main, the tributary and the outlet) in the very same juxtaposition and co-relation they were in from 1578 to 1830, the only difference being that the meeting place of the three rivers has been transferred a few miles eastward of the old bend, for the simple reason that, not feeling able to cope with our gigantic river, nor to accomplish the super-human task of forcing it back again in the old channel it occupied three hundred years ago, we have taken the much more easily managed small streams (the Red and the Atchafalaya rivers) by the hand, as it were, and led them into a direct communication and contact with the Mississippi, so that, by said operations, once more, and as in olden times (compare plates No. 1. and No. 4.), the tributary (Red River) empties its waters directly in the main river,

and the outlet (the Atchafalaya) receives its waters directly from
the main river, which being accomplished, the danger of the Red
and Atchafalaya becoming separated from the Mississippi river is
overcome and at an end, and the question, "how to secure in a
permanent manner the water connection of said three streams," is
satisfactorily answered.

It is hoped and believed that, in the course of the above remarks,
it has been demonstrated in almost a tangible manner how the
dangers very rightfully apprehended by the signers of the above-
mentioned petition to the Governor can be averted, and how the
boon of a healthy and permanent navigable communication between
the Mississippi and the fertile territory of Western Louisiana can be
permanently secured; it is also believed that, after such a clear and forcible statement of facts, it would be useless and a most futile to dwell
upon and attempt to urge the necessity of carrying out the works of
improvement delineated in plate No. 3; and, therefore, hoping that
the problem of "How to prevent the closing up navigable communication between the Red and the Mississippi rivers?" has been
satisfactorily solved,   I remain, very respectfully,

E. H. ANGAMAR,

Of the Board of State Engineers.

In George T. Dunbar's report to the Board of Public Works of
Louisiana, made in the year 1840, in speaking of the closing of Old
River, he says:

In making a report upon this subject, I hold it entirely useless to
advance theories and opinions.   Volumes might be written to sup-
port different opinions, and many sound arguments advanced, but the
conclusion would be that the party which had made no examination
of the effects produced, would find itself farther from a right view
of the subject than ever.   I shall, therefore, to avoid the contro-
versy attendant upon conflicting opinions, confine myself, as nearly
as possible to my observations, and merely state the facts as they
occur.

By referring to my report upon this subject laid before you in
May last, it will be found that on the eighteenth day of January, 1839,
we had five and a half feet water over the bar at the mouth of Red
River, five and a half feet water on the bar in the Atchafalaya,

eighteen inches say over the bar at the lower mouth, and ten feet over the bar in the upper mouth ; showing a difference of four and a half feet between the bar in the upper mouth, and the bar in the Atchafalaya.

On the 13th of February, 1839, we had ten feet water over the bar at the mouth of Red River, seventeen feet in the upper mouth with no current, twelve and a half feet in the mouth of the Atchafalaya, with a strong current, and four and a half feet over the bar at the lower mouth, showing an increase of deposits on the bar at Red River of two feet, and one of three and a half feet on the bar at the lower mouth, while the relative depths of the Atchafalaya and the upper mouth remained the same. This estimate was based upon the supposition that the bar in the Atchafalaya, being composed of hard blue clay, would not cut by the action of the water.

By my examinations this season we have the following results: The main part of the lower mouth was two and a half feet out of water, the balance was entirely dry, with the exception of a small communication about ten feet wide (vide plan A) on a level with the surface of the water. The soundings show a depth of seven and a half feet in the channel over the bar in the upper mouth (vide plan A,) six inches water on the shoalest part of the bar at Red river (vide plan B,) and five and a half feet on the bar in the Atchafalaya (vide plan C.) The present difference then between the bars in the upper mouth and the Atchafalaya is two feet; making a decrease of difference between the two of two and a half feet since January last.

I am inclined to believe that the bed of the Atchafalaya is cutting, but having no fixed point by which I could test it, I am unable to say positively that it has cut; however, by far the greater portion of the differences has been caused by deposits. The navigation has been exceedingly favored by our not having any high water in the Mississippi, but still, low as the water has been, the deposits at the various points have been enormous.

The dark-colored portion of the island in front of Bishop's landing (vide plan A) is the only portion which was visible during the low water of 1838; since then the island has extended to the position marked upon the plan, being entirely closed below. In the space comprehended between the point of this island (A) and the bar opposite (G), we had during the low stage of water in 1838 upwards

2

of thirty feet water. The same stage this season would have given scant thirteen feet in the deepest part. By examining the pass A (plan A), we find a narrow channel with thirty-six feet water, showing the effort of Red River to seek the deep water of the Mississippi; with what success this effort was met, the bar, to which I have just referred, will best explain. The deposit was cut from the pass and precipitated immediately below, making a nucleus upon which the mighty river is fast forming its banks. I now turn the attention of the board to plan B: By an accurate observation of the soundings and profile of the river, marked F to G (vide plan D), we are led to believe that Old River in this neighborhood is contracting for the purpose of affording a narrow channel for Red River. We find at F a channel only three hundred feet wide, averaging forty feet in depth. Following the line of soundings from F toward the Atchafalaya, and we discover between the points E and A the bold outline of the great bar which is forming, and which seems to me to be the chief obstruction we have to encounter. On this line, immediately under the small island A, we find twenty-seven feet water, but by referring to the soundings and profile from F to G and from G to snag O, we discover that this channel loses itself on the shoal below. On the line from A to D, immediately across and in the mouth of Red River, we find the deepest water beyond the outline or summit of the bar, and in direction of the Atchafalaya, and by examining the different lines of sounding along and across the bar, we see the depth change suddenly from thirteen feet to seventy-six feet towards the Atchafalaya.

That this bar must increase so as to close the channel without having a space for Red River is evident, as otherwise the deposit would never have formed a regular line E to A, but would have left a very deep channel at E. When the waters of the Mississippi are up, there is no contending force to oppose them in passing through their old channel until they reach this point, and here the greater portion of the sediment must be precipitated. The question is often asked why has not this been done before? I conceive that the question has no bearing whatever upon the matters before us. Previous to the cut-off being made, the Atchafalaya had not, nor could have any effect upon it. But after the cut-off was made the influence of the Atchafalaya was felt. A firm barrier was thrown across the upper month, the Atchafalaya afforded a passage for the water of Red River and a bar was soon formed across the lower mouth. Now the increase of these bars is daily weakening the force of Red River as regards its contention with the Mississippi, and at the same time rendering the Atchafalaya a more powerful agent in destroying the communication of Red River with the Mississippi.

I will now turn the attention of the board to plan C, showing the plan, soundings, and profiles of the first mile and three-quarters of the Atchafalaya. The contrast exhibited at the first glance between the deep waters and the shoal, together with the position of the mouth, would induce any one to pronounce, unhesitatingly, the impossibility of Red River going down the Atchafalaya. Upon examination of the profile, it will be found that, with the exception of the small bar at the mouth, and the bar at the Coville, the whole map is nothing more than a bank of soft mud, and that in the event of the removal of the bar at the Coville, we would have very deep water from the bar at the mouth down. As a proof of this, Mr. John Harmonson, a long resident on the island, states that during the low water of 1830 and 1831, there was a raft of logs in the Atchafalaya half barred in the mud. The Coville was suddenly swelled by heavy rain, the timber forced into Old River, and a channel seventeen feet in depth cut where the timber rested. It will also be noticed that the mouth is daily changing its position. The position marked in red, and exhibiting a long narrow neck of land, was a few years since as high as the main land; now it is only a few feet above low water, with numerous breaks in the bank. The capability of the Atchafalaya to vent the water of the Red River is without doubt, the section being much larger than at the Rapions. The opinion that the Atchafalaya was a portion of, or, in other words, the old channel of Red River, seems to me to be erroneous. This opinion is based upon the fact that the geological formation is very similar to that of Red River, but it must be remembered that during high water very little of the Red River water ever flowed beyond it. Again, if we examine the profile, we find it bearing evidence that the Atchafalaya owes its depth at the mouth entirely to the abrasion of the banks by the Mississippi.

This argument, however, has been opposed by supposing the raft in the Atchafalaya to have caused the deposit in the mouth. The raft could not have had this effect without the sediment first filling in its own neighborhood. This has not been done, for there is no place in the Atchafalaya after we pass the first mile and three-quarters where the water is not deeper than across the mouth of Red River. Again, one of the oldest settlers in the neighborhood states that, about twenty years since, he rode across the Atchafalaya at low water, and found the banks, or bed, to be full eight feet above the surface of the Mississippi. This goes strongly to show that its depth is caused by the inroads of the Mississippi. But the most conclusive evidence which I can offer upon this subject is a survey of the River Mississippi, or "St. Louis," made by order of the French government during 1715 to 1725 by the sieur Xiron. This chart has never been published, but a copy of it was obtained by the late Joseph M. White, Esq., to whom I am indebted for the copy in my possession. This survey shows the changes in this neighborhood to have been very great and wonderful. The Atchafalaya has no communication whatever with the Mississippi. The river, instead of running southwest past the mouth of Red River, runs south, 20 deg. east across the present island. In the channel of the stream existed two islands, forming what was called les trois Chenaux. As to the truth of the survey, I can vouch for it; I have examined the island and found evidences of the channels alluded to.

The hope that the channel of Old Red river would fill up part the mouth of the Atchafalaya before any serious injury could be done to the navigation of Red River I consider vain. The barrier across the lower mouth gains several feet in height every season, and as it gains, the channel beyond will be less affected by the Mississippi; no instance can be cited of the filling of any low ground beyond a high bank. The bank destroys the current, and precipitates the sediment upon and immediately around it. From the results shown by my examinations, we arrive at the following conclusions: First, the deposits will cause a long extended bar, leaving barely depth for the boats to pass in low water. Second, That the bar will increase to such an extent as to cause the destruction of the low water navigation, but still leave a passage for a great portion of the water. Third, That the mouths will close entirely, and force the water to seek its outlet in the Atchafalaya.

In either case the low water navigation of the Atchafalaya is made; let the bar increase but two feet and we will have six feet over the bar in the Atchafalaya in dead low water. I pretend not to give any decisive opinion as to the ultimate result; indeed I feel that it can not be done; the examination of another season may produce entirely different results. One high water in the Mississippi will decide the matter. We well know that, contrary to all theory, all expectation, and all experience, the upper mouth closed long before the lower. The cause still exists, and what has been done can and may be done again. We can not pretend to contend against the cause, but we can counteract the effects. In dismissing this important subject I have to request that the board will allow me to continue my examinations at this point at such times as I may deem necessary. I have established points and levels, to enable me at any time to ascertain the precise changes which may take place.

In the report made by Charles Ellet, on the Mississippi and Ohio rivers, made in 1853, under the auspices of the United States, when speaking of the enlargement of the Atchafalaya, he says:

The Atchafalaya is by far the largest of the existing or former outlets of the Mississippi; and it has been often proposed to resort to its channel as the best and most efficient drain for the floods which now threaten the country below its source.

In concurring with this popular idea, so far as to advise a commencement of the gradual and progressive enlargement of this great stream, it is not intended to represent the work as easy to accomplish, or in itself an effectual remedy for the floods of lower Louisiana.

It will, in fact, be found to be an exceedingly difficult and costly undertaking, and one which will need to be conducted cautiously and not too rapidly, if it is to be effected without serious injury to the region through which the waters are to be conveyed.

The Atchafalaya leaves the old channel of the Mississippi about two miles below the mouth of Red River, and 310 miles, by the windings of the channel, above the Gulf of Mexico. It flows nearly in a southwardly direction; and when the Mississippi is swollen by floods, it serves as a natural vent for a portion of the present excess of waters, of which it bears off a large volume to the sea.

At its source its average surface width in extreme high water is about 600 feet; its depth fifty-five feet; its slope six inches per mile; and its discharge not less than 85,000 cubic feet per second. It is about equal, measured by the area of its channel and the volume of water which it conveys, to *one-twelfth part* of the capacity of the Mississippi above New Orleans.

It has long been supposed that the Atchafalaya was the ancient bed of Red River, when that stream had no connection with the Mississippi, but found its way to the Gulf of Mexico by an independent channel. The union of the two streams—the Mississippi and Red River—is accounted for, in this theory, by the supposition that, at the point where their waters now mingle, their channels then exhibited opposing flexures, and the current gradually cutting away the intervening soil, brought the streams together and made their waters common.

This has become of late years a very popular theory, and is supported by several plausible arguments. The position of the mouth of Red River on the one hand, and that of the source of the Atchafalaya on the other; the direction by which Red River enters, and that by which the Atchafalaya leaves the old channel of the Mississippi correspond perfectly with the assumption that the curves of the two adjacent streams gradually approached, until they finally cut into each other. Besides, the color of the soil composing the west bank of the Atchafalaya at its source indicates clearly a Red River origin. But, notwithstanding the plausibility and force of these facts, they are not at all conclusive, but apply with equal directness to another view that will be here suggested.

In fact, the hypothesis which attributes the original formation of the Atchafalaya to the discharge of Red River is found, on a careful examination, to be wholly untenable. It results from actual measurements of the channels of these two rivers; that while the Atchafalaya at its source has a prevailing depth at high water, in mid-channel way, of only about fifty-five feet, Red River, at its mouth, only three miles distant, exhibits a depth of more than one hundred feet; that, while the Atchafalaya is confined within a channel less than six hundred feet wide at its surface, in high water the width of Red River, between banks, a mile above its mouth, is more than 1100 feet; and that, while the descent of the Atchafalaya at or near its mouth is six inches per mile, that of Red River, where it enters Old River, is at low water less than one inch per mile.

The hypothesis of a former continuous channel, common to these two streams, so different in all their features, must, therefore, concede a sudden and remarkable change in the character of the supposed ancient Red River, at the precise point of the present junction of that stream with the Mississippi. Such a change, and the exact coincidence of that change with the point of accidental contact of the two shifting channels is, indeed, not impossible, but it is, at least quite improbable. A less violent and much more satisfactory theory, to account for the existence of the Atchafalaya—one of the most remarkable features of the Mississippi—may be suggested, though the writer has not had full opportunities to submit it to a very rigid inspection.

Black River, the proper continuation of the Ouachita, corresponds much more closely in the dimensions of its channel with those of the Atchafalaya than Red River. The general direction of the Ouachita is from north to south, corresponding well with the present general course of the Atchafalaya.

The idea has impressed itself upon the mind of the writer, that in the original condition of the delta, the Ouachita, as well as Red River, descended by an independent channel to the Gulf, which then, perhaps, set up through a bay as far as the head of Lake Chicot.

The Mississippi at that period pursued its present general direction. Red River had also its own independent channel to the Gulf, in the present valley of the Teche, where it has left abundant traces of its course, in the composition of the soil and in the width and form of the immediate valley of the present stream from above the rapids at Alexandria down to Berwick's Bay. The Ouachita was thus an independent stream descending to the sea between Red River and the Mississippi.

According to this hypothesis, the Ouachita and the Mississippi, by the gradual approach of opposite bends, ultimately united their waters, and the Ouachita was, so to speak, cut in two—the northern part afterwards serving as a feeder to the Mississippi, and the Southern end acting as an outlet for its surplus water in times of flood.

The Ouachita having been a stream of smaller class than Red River, may be adduced as a reason why the present channel of the Atchafalaya, which was formed to accommodate the volume which that river, and not Red River, brought down, is insufficient for the discharge of the present volume of Red River. The Ouachita flowing directly down the plane of the delta, which it has been shown, descends at the rate of eight inches per mile, accounts for the greater fall of the Atchafalaya which takes the same direction parallel with the dip of the same plane.

Subsequently to the junction of Ouachita and the Mississippi, Red River—then continuing on below Alexandria in the same southeasterly direction which it still pursues above that point—flowed over its natural levee, and, taking an easterly direction through the swamps, united its waters with those of the Ouachita at the present month of the Black River. Under this hypothesis, the increased volume below the confluence of these streams, in the course of thousands of years, may have produced the larger channel known as Red River, which even now is scarcely sufficient to accomodate their collected waters.

According to this view, which is suggested as the most plausible explanation of the existence of the Atchafalaya, that stream was the ancient channel of the Ouachita, or its prolongation, Black River; and the present channel of Red River, below the mouth of Black, was subsequently enlarged by the union of the waters of the Red and Black.

These considerations are not without a practical value in the present discussion.

If it be true that the Ouachita had an ancient independent outlet through the Atchafalaya, the fact that this outlet has not increased in capactiy since its function has been to give passage to the waters of the Mississippi, which it conveys to the sea-level by a slope twice as great as that of the Mississippi itself, is further evidence that the apprehension so often expressed, that it may ultimately absorb the Mississippi, is without reasonable foundation.

In fact, it is not yet demonstrated that this outlet may not have been one of those original vents which, like the Plaquemines, Manchac, and Lafourche, and numerous other bayous, were formed, as the outlets near the mouth of the river are now formed during the deposition of the soil, and for the purpose of relieving the channel of its high water load. Be that as it may, the Atchafalaya has existed for ages, and now exhibits signs rather of a progressive contraction than an enlargement of its area. There is, in fact, not only no reason to believe that it will ever open its own channel wider and deeper, but scarcely even substantial ground to hope that this result can be materially promoted by any moderate amount of cost or labor.

The Atchafalaya, at its source, draws from the Mississippi, in very high floods, about 85,000 cubic feet of water per second, or

about eight per cent. of the actual discharge of the main channel
of the river. But the right or west bank of the bayou, is overflowed
in high floods by the back water of the Mississippi, or by that of
the Red River ; and below the mouth of bayou Des Glaize, five
miles from the source of the Atchafalaya, the extreme high water
discharges, constantly increased by accession from Red River, to
about 140,000 cubic feet per second—or thirteen per cent., of the
total discharge of the main channel of the river.*

No observation was obtained at the time of extreme highwater.

It is by observing these accessions from Red River, when the
Mississippi has begun to fall, and the confined water of Red River
obtains vent, that we are enabled to account for that red deposit on
the west bank of the bayou, which has been so long regarded as conclusive evidence that this was once the proper channel of Red River itself.
While the bayou is drawing in the water of the Mississippi at its source,
the water of Red River, charged with its characteristic deposit, and
deeply colored, flows rapidly through the swamps and pours over
the whole west bank of the Atchafalaya for a space of four or five
miles, from Old River down to Simmsport, and slowly mingles with
that of the Mississippi. It is from this Red River overflow that the
west bank of the Atchafalaya receives the red stain. But the overflow from that quarter diminishes as we descend, and a red deposit
becomes also less and less clearly defined.

In this, the upper part of its source, the Atchafalaya may be
easily and cheaply enlarged. The purpose may be effected by first
cultivating its borders and clearing off all vegetable growth, and
then cutting down the salient points, and encouraging the action of
the water upon them. The difficulty, however, of converting the
stream into an efficient outlet is not found here at its source, but in-
creases from mile to mile as it descends, until it discharges itself, by
numerous mouths into Grand river; and again, through numerous
bayous, leading from that river into the lakes which intervene between it and the Gulf.

The real difficulty consists in the fact, that the Atchafalaya loses
its importance and its power as it advances below the Bayou des
Glaize. It yields the water which it had drawn from the Missis-

---

* When the Atchafalaya was gauged (April 26, 1850), the water had fallen at its source to
two feet two inches. The actual discharge was then found to be—
At its source..77,100 cubic feet per second.
Below Bayou Des Glaize...122,700 cubic feet per second.

sippi and Red River to numerous outlets, which diverge from it to the right and left; and, as it received accessions from Red River, which were discharged into it from the swamps above, so it discharges them again over its banks into the swamps of the interior below.

In passing down this stream in the latter part of April, 1851, when its surface had fallen 2.2 feet from its extreme high water mark of that year, at Old river, and one foot at the head of Grand river, and gauging its volume from point to point, the following results were obtained:

Cubic feet:

The Atchafalaya drew from the Mississippi, at its source, in Old River, per second.... 77,100

It received accessions from Red River in the first five miles, which increased the discharge to, per second 122,700

At a point one mile above the raft the losses caused by lateral drains had reduced the discharge to, per second.. 88,600

At Pickets, one mile below Bayou Rouge and Bayou Latanache, its volume had been reduced down to, per second 67,900

At a point just below the source of Alabama bayou, it was found to be only, per second 41,870

Nine miles below the mouth of Bayou Little Devil, and half a mile below the re-entrance of Bayou Alabama, the discharge of this great stream had dwindled down to, per second 19,400

In addition to the effect of these continual losses, by which its volume is reduced to less than the sixth part of that which its channel discharged at Simmsport, the power of the current in this outlet is still further reduced by a corresponding change in its rate of descent.

The actual descent in the lower part of the course of the stream was not measured, but the velocity was frequently tested; and, compared with the observations taken in the first twenty miles below Old River, they showed a falling off in the speed of the current of nearly one-half.

To make the main channel of the Atchafalaya capable of accomodating the volume of water which even now enters from above, the remaining obstruction at the raft must first be removed, and the capacity of the stream must be increased an average of fully three fold its present value, for a distance of forty miles. If, therefore, it should be attempted, as has been suggested, to produce the enlargement by pouring in more water at the source of this outlet in Old River, without first preparing the channels below to give it vent, we shall overflow a great extent of country, and retard for years, if not permanently, its proper and necessary drainage.

This is one of those cases in which every consideration of prudence and economy urges the commencement of the works of reclamation and enlargement below.

The Atchafalaya and Plaquemines discharge their waters at the opposite extremities, and through various bayous, at intermediate points along the course of Grand River. This river is now, in fact, the recipient of all the water of overflow, and the crevasse water, together with that of the natural outlets of the Mississippi and Red River, from the source of the Plaquemines to the Red River rapids. The water thus received by Grand River from so many sources is discharged from it through numerous bayous and small lakes into Lake Chicot and Grand Lake. These bayous are very crooked and frequently obstructed. Their descent is small, and the current passing through them is, in many places, extremely sluggish. If the enlargement of the Atchafalaya be undertaken, these bayous must be simultaneously relieved of obstructions to the passage of water through them, and straightened and enlarged, so that the additional volume of water received by Grand River may flow more readily into the lakes, and not spread over, and forever destroy, the great area of swamps yet reclaimable by which these lakes are surrounded. The work of enlargement may then proceed upward along all the bayous which now drain the Atchafalaya, and which will still be required to vent the greatly increased volume that is to be conveyed.

It is not to be supposed that this work can be effected speedily, at trifling cost, or without involving much local damage. The accomplishment of the labor, so as to produce appreciable results, will require several years, however ample the means may be, or with whatever vigor the work be pressed, and a portion of the country will inevitably be flooded, however prudently its execution may proceed.

It was no part of the duty of the writer to investigate in detail the damages that may accrue from the accomplishment of this plan.

It was sufficient to see and to know that the preservation of great interests from destruction will ultimately compel a resort to this measure. And, as it is clearly in the power of those who control the progress of the work to arrest it, whenever the damage threatened is about to exceed the value of the results produced, it seems unnecessary to delay it for minute and doubtful estimates.

But, as already intimated, the enlargement of the Atchafalaya by any justifiable process, will prove to be a slow and expensive undertaking, involving great labor and loss of life. The work, therefore, though necessary and proper to be commenced, will not afford that prompt relief which is demanded by the present emergency. The country needs immediate protection against actual distress, and effectual guarantees against approaching dangers. For these we must look to the Plaquemines as the only point, on the west side of the river, at which we can relieve the lower coast with the necessary dispatch. Another outlet will be presently suggested, in case of great emergency, as a temporary expedient; but the Plaquemines is, beyond all comparison, the channel by which we can most confidently undertake to produce visible and valuable results for moderate cost and with the necessary rapidity.

The Atchafalaya, when enlarged, will be much the most important outlet that can be obtained; because it draws off the water at the highest accessible point on the river. It is, therefore, not to be neglected; but is recommended here as a place at which the work should be commenced without delay.

In the report of Professor C. G. Forshey to the Senate Committee of Louisiana, in 1850, he writes:

To the Hon. S. Ricker:

In the surveys of the Atchafalaya basin and channels, you directed us to inquire into the practicability of increasing the discharge from the Mississippi and Red rivers through these channels to the Gulf of Mexico.

The original survey of August was not carried sufficiently far down to satisfy us upon this subject, and the engineers in the company were nearly equally divided in opinion upon this subject. For my own part, you will remember that I was opposed to expressing an opinion for want of information.

Subsequently, I completed the investigation by a series of surveys, levels and transverse measurements of channels, which left nothing to be directed in this respect.

I found the level of the Grand Lake, at the high-water mark of 1850, almost precisely four feet above the level of the Atchafalaya Bay, at low tide of eighteen inches, distance thirty miles, or about 1.6 inches per mile.

In 1851, the water rose only to a point 1.5 feet below the mark of 1850, which gave it a fall from Grand Lake of 2.5 feet, or one inch per mile, to the Gulf; or at high tide 1 4 feet, giving .5 inch per mile.

In 1828, and prior thereto, when there were few levees, and the water flowed thither at its option, the water mark was 6.6 feet higher than the present mean tide. This was nearly equal to the highest lands, and most of the banks of the lower Teche, Atchafalaya and Berwick's Bay were submerged. It then had a fall of 2.6 inches per mile, equal to the Mississippi, from Red River down.

Now, the Berwick's Bay and a bayou called Bœuf, draining Lake Pallourde, from the whole outlet of the Atchafalaya basin:

	Square Feet.
Berwick's Bay has a sectional area of	104,219
And Bayou Bœuf......	10,146
Total discharging capacity (1850)	114,365
In 1828, when the water was 3.5 feet higher	123,600
The total capacity of the Mississippi	168,200

The capacity of the Atchafalaya outlets are then seventy-five per cent. of the Mississippi at Carrollton.

At the elevation of Grand Lake, in 1828, the current would run through its channels at the same velocity as the Mississippi river—namely, at 2.60 miles per hour, 3.80 feet per second, and would discharge a quantity of water equal to three-fourths of the river's discharge; and would maintain the channel, which that habitual velocity carved there, resembling in form very much the Mississippi proper.

At the elevation of Grand Lake in 1850—when it was forty-two inches lower than 1828, leaving only half the declivity—the section would be contracted only 6,300 square feet, or five per cent.; and yet its discharging capacity, measured by the velocities for like declivity in the Mississippi river, would be reduced one-fourth, or twenty-five per cent.

The present state of the bottom of both these channels is such as to prove that they are rapidly filling up. The soft mud at the bottom, into which a lead will sink several feet, is indicative of the sluggishness of the currents which flow through them.

These are the facts. What are the natural inferences? I deduce these:

First—The channels produced by the waters formerly discharged at a high velocity through them are closing of themselves since the reduction of the overflow level of Grand Lake and of the basin.

Second—This filling up is from sediment of river water since the retardation of the velocity due to a greater fall of water.

Third—Any attempt to produce other or greater channels of discharge for the waters in this basin, unless by elevating the level of the lake and increasing the velocity of the currents, must prove utterly fruitless, as these, too, would fill up with sedimentary matter.

Fourth—The crevasses of 1858, amounting to five miles in length, and 5.3 feet mean depth, and sectional area of 140,000 square feet, did not elevate the lakes sufficiently to scour out the soft mud in the channels of outlet, though they were sufficient to inundate a vast region of cultivated lands, and produce the most afflicting disasters.

Fifth—These lakes, and the Atchafalaya basin, need no increase of outlet. They need head or elevation above the Gulf, and nothing else will be of any service. It remains for the people on the margin of that basin to say if they can bear a higher water than 1850. I think not!

And, if the State is to profit in any degree by the valuable domain of swamp land which has been donated to her; or, if she would build roads, and inhabit and cultivate her territories, it would seem wanton to resubmerge the lands reclaimed, and subject the remaining country to increased inundations.

There is no mode of controlling those waters after their departure from the river, or the channels might possibly be made to hold and discharge the necessary waters.

In the report of A. D. Wooldridge, State Engineer, in the year 1852, he says of Red River :

Red River is navigable for fifteen hundred miles from its junction with the Mississippi. It runs through, perhaps, the best cotton region in the United States. In its ample and fertile valley will, ere long, be produced, not only immense quantities of cotton and sugar, but of grains, tobacco, cattle, etc.

It will be the locality of towns and villages innumerable, and its commerce alone, if concentrated, will be sufficient to sustain a great city. Were this river thoroughly improved, from the Mississippi to its highest navigable point, it would offer the best field for enterprising and industrious agriculturists to be found in the United States. Far beyond the present frontier settlements, its vast and rich valley extends itself, offering to the settler as good land as any in the world for even less, in many instances, than one dollar per acre. It has rich land, a fine climate, a healthy locality, undeveloped wealth beyond computation ; everything but a reliable and successful navigation. But acknowledging, as we must, the great results to be derived from the thorough improvement of this stream, the important question arises, how far its improvement can, or ought to be effected by Louisiana alone ?

It is a stream in which not only Louisiana is interested, but Arkansas, Texas, and the whole country extending to the feet of the Rocky Mountains. It is a national stream, and deserves the fostering care of the nation. There is a school of politicians in the country who are opposed to governmental expenditures for internal improvements ; but, if I mistake not, the best teachers in that school have had compass of mind enough to discriminate between works of a merely local character and those of great national importance. The former may with propriety be left to the several States, but the latter being of great general utility and requiring vast amounts for their construction, need the aid of the strong arm of the general government.

Entertaining these views, and feeling the great importance of the thorough improvement of Red River throughout its whole navigable course, I would respectfully suggest to the Legislature the propriety of uniting with Arkansas, Texas, and other States, who would aid in the matter, in asking of Congress an appropriation for the permanent improvement of this stream. The work is beyond our means, and delays are not only injurious, but may be dangerous.

Louis Hebert, State Engineer, in 1856, says :

The navigation of this stream has been for a time almost entirely cut off during the year by the low stage of the water. The want of depth of water has been felt throughout the entire stream, but more particularly in that part of Old River which is the only connection of Red River with the Mississippi. Here, as it has been feared by many, bars have formed which threaten soon and completely to separate the two rivers. A thorough survey of the mouths of the Atchafalaya and Red River and of Old River, made in January, 1855, and another survey made in September of this year, by Mr. L. A. Wrotnowski, prove that very important and rapid changes have occurred in Old River, and that everything is tending to throw the Red River down the Atchafalaya. In my opinion, we see here at last but a natural result hastened on by the old Shreve cut-off and, more recently, by the Raccourci cut-off. From the time of Shreve's cut-off, the new bed of the Mississippi, made by said cut-off, has been gradually gaining east, and leaving Red River to the west, thus lengthening the distance and, therefore, reducing the plane of inclination of the Red River waters. Naturally, the waters have sought the Atchafalaya. The Raccourci cut-off, by increasing the abrasion of the banks of the Mississippi, has tended materially to hasten the course of this stream eastward.

It is my settled conviction that Red river will separate itself from the Mississippi, and find its way to the sea by the Atchafalaya, unless something is done by mankind to prevent such a result. Now, the question is, "Shall we prevent this result, and if we do, in what way is it to be done?" In the first place, "Shall we prevent it?" There is no doubt that Berwick's Bay affords a very good harbor, and its shores a beautiful location for a commercial city. Therefore, there would be no difficulty in finding a mart for the new artery opened for the Red river trade. Again, Red river being the most southern tributary of the Mississippi of any importance, its floods have naturally the greatest influence on the overflows of the last stream throughout lower Louisiana. On the other hand, will New Orleans consent to loose the commerce of the Red river and of the entire west of the State, and see a rival, in State commerce at least, grow up on Berwick's Bay? It will cost much to turn again the Red River water in the Mississippi. It can however be done. And here comes the question, "In what way is it to be done?" It is evident that we must separate Red River from the Atchafalaya. We can not close the Atchafalaya, nor would any partial closing be advisable, nor of any permanent effect.

The only safe way perhaps is to open a passage to the Red River through what is known as Cut-off Bayou, and closing the river just below the bayou. This has been suggested to me by my assistant,

Mr. L. J. Frémaux, but I find that Mr. George T. Dunbar, Engineer of the Board of Public Works in 1839, entertained the same object. I am not prepared to say that this would cost less than the estimate of Mr. Dunbar, ($2,000,000) but the matter is important enough for the consideration of your honorable bodies and of the Internal Improvement Department.

Nothing has been done, I believe, during the year, upon the falls at Alexandria. In my annual report I strongly recommended the construction of locks upon one or the other falls. I must here repeat my recommendation. *Nothing else will do*, and the large commerce of Red River (large even now, and increasing so as to be at some day almost incalculable,) warrants any outlay, even to millions of dollars.

In 1860, J. K. Duncan, the then Chief Engineer of the Board of Public Works, made an elaborate report, and as he quotes from Louis Hébert much of his reports, we have concluded to let his report cover both, and apologize for not giving Colonel Hebert's report. Duncan says:

In pursuance of instructions from the Board of Public Works, I examined and made the necessary surveys of Old River, the mouth of the Red, and the head, or source of the Atchafalaya rivers, together with such parts of those streams and their tributaries and of the adjacent country, as I considered involved in any way, in properly complying with the requirements of the following acts of 1859 and 1860, to wit:

First.—Act No. 262, of 1859, appropriates thirty-five thousand dollars "For the purpose of preserving the navigation of the Old River, between the mouth of Red River and the Mississippi, and also to make such examinations and surveys as may be required to establish the works necessary to prevent a separation of the Red and Mississippi rivers."

Second.—Joint resolution No. 29, of 1860, "Requires the Board of Public Works to examine and report to the Legislature as early as practicable, as to the utility and practicability, and the cost of constructing a levee or dam across Old River, through which Red River communicates with the Atchafalaya River, and to report upon the effects of this work upon the Mississippi River."

Third.—Joint resolution No. 30, of 1860, "Requires the board to examine and report to the Legislature as early as practicable, as to

the practicability and probable cost of partially closing the mouth of
the Atchafalaya River on the Old River, so as to reduce the present
width of the Atchafalaya to the width of sixty feet, or so much as is
necessary not to obstruct navigation, and to report upon the effects
that such dam will have upon the Mississippi river."

These acts are similar in their import, but differ materially in
their extent and consequences.

The first proposes to effect a permanent improvement of the navigation of Old River, and thus continually to keep open, through
its channels, the communication of the Red River with the Mississippi.

The second literally calls for the effects likely to be produced
upon the Mississippi only by the experiment of throwing a dam
across Old River below the mouth of Red River.

And the third proposes in a like manner to determine the probable effects produced upon the Mississippi by a partial closing of the
head of the Atchafalaya.

The first act indicates plainly an important object; whereas the
second and third, only invites speculation and theory, which will
prove as little beneficial to the Legislator, as to the Engineer. It
is obvious, however, that the main object of this and of previous
Legislation has been to solve the difficult problem of keeping. permanently open the low water navigation through Old River, as a
common communication for both the Red and the Atchafalaya rivers
with the Mississippi. This is one of the most important problems,
perhaps, which can be presented to the people of Louisiana, as it not
only embraces the question of low water navigation under discussion, but its successful solution, which can be accomplished in but
one way alone, but is also the key to a perfect system of reclamation
and drainage for a large part of the State. Its physical difficulties,
however, are of the highest order, and its solution involves so many
elements, that a brief history of the causes and effects leading to the
present embarrassed condition of things, is absolutely required in
order to a clear understanding of the subject in hand.

ORIGIN AND CAUSES OF THE DETERIORATION OF THE NAVIGATION OF OLD RIVER.

I am unwilling to admit a mere speculation in this report, but in
as far as the question of original unity between the Red and the

Atchafalaya rivers is concerned, this is unavoidable. History and tradition, at the remotest dates, found the same indirect separation of these rivers as there is at present; for, no direct evidence of a more perfect connection between them has ever come down to our times. Hence our deductions regarding this former unity can now only be based upon a careful inspection of the present geography and geology of the valleys of the two rivers in question. A close examination and comparison of the physical aspects and the geological formations of these valleys, leads one inevitably to the conclusion that there was a former time when the Red and Atchafalaya rivers were one and the same stream, which had no connection with the Mississippi whatever, except through lateral overflows in extreme floods. It is not presumed by this, that there were not other outlets to Red River besides the Atchafalaya, during the outward progress of the whole front of its delta.

The Teche, in all probability, was such an outlet up to a very recent period comparatively. But upon due investigation of the subject, however, the conviction will force itself upon every one, that, as the land extended outward, the Atchafalaya became the final and only remaining one of these outlets.

I am aware that this former unity between the Red and the Atchafalaya rivers has been questioned by several able and scientific writers. The problem of low water navigation, which remains to be solved, however, depends upon the present existence of things, and not upon the changes of the past; and, therefore, it is immaterial whether this premise be admitted or not, as it will be fully proven hereafter that these two rivers form one and the same stream now, which will be sufficient for our argument. The Red and the Mississippi rivers then occupied separate valleys, running generally parallel with each other, but with no immediate connection between them. The latter sought the Gulf at the Balize through its own independent channel, while the former reached the sea through the Atchafalaya and Berwick's Bay.

The general tendency of alluvial streams is ever to lengthen their courses and reduce their slopes. As a consequence of the tortuous meanderings resulting from this consideration, the Red and Mississippi rivers came together and mingled their waters. In thus coming together, however, it must be borne steadily in mind that the former was completely cut into two parts; and that the bend or loop of the Mississippi, now called Old River, separated these parts by a distance of about three miles, and thus maintained an indirect communication only between them. For easy nomenclature, we will designate these parts by the names by which they are now known: that is, we will call the upper one Red River, and the lower the Atchafalaya.

The annexed diagram (Figure I) illustrates the probable position of the Red and Mississippi rivers, a short time previous to their meeting; and (Figure II.) their absolute condition subsequent to the making of Shreve's and the Raccourci's cut-offs.

EFFECTS OF THE MEETING.

The natural effects which would be produced by the meeting of the waters of the Red and Mississippi rivers would be as follows :

Effects upon the Atchafalaya.—As the Atchafalaya flowed directly from the apex of an abrupt bend of the Mississippi, which then, as now, constituted its source or head, it is evident that, after the meeting mentioned, it would become the general recipient of most of the floating drift coming down the Mississippi during the rise of its floods. The inevitable result of this would be the complete rafting of the Atchafalaya from Berwick's Bay to its head. Everything proves this dense rafting to have taken place, traces of which are apparent throughout the entire course of the river, in its lake formation, and in its numerous lateral chutes, caused by the water breaking around the rafts and coming in again below them. This has been known to be the case up to a very recent date, as but a few years have elapsed since the rafts were broken and removed by the Internal Department.

These obstructions would render the current of the Atchafalaya very sluggish, whence there would be a consequent rapid deposition of sediment upon the rafts, causing the channel of the river to contract and shoal its bed.

This co-relation between the transporting velocity of the channel of an alluvial stream, and the inertia and cohesion of the bottom and sides of its channel are self-evident. If water be taken from the muddiest stream and allowed to become quiescent in a vessel, it at once precipitates the earthy matter in suspension and becomes pure and limpid, because this sediment had been lifted and carried along entirely by the velocity of the current, or the mechanical action of water in motion. We have similar results in all sedimentary streams, wherein the slightest check of the current will produce a corresponding deposit in the channel immediately at the point where the current is checked.

The converse of this is equally true, that the matter of an alluvial stream will be filled or saturated with earthy matter in suspension directly in proportion to the increase of the velocity of its current. A mountain torrent, for instance, detaches last fragments of rocks and rounds them into pebbles by the force of its current alone.

Such a current, in many of the streams of Louisiana, would carray away bodily large masses of earth. Besides the fact is familiar to every one, that the water of the Mississippi is more free from sediment at its low stages, than it is during the increased velocity of its floods.

These universal hydro-dynamical laws are dwelt upon in this connection, because their effects are not sufficiently considered in constructing many of the works of the State, and because we will have occasion to refer to them frequently in this report hereafter.

Effects on the Red River.—It is plain that when their waters first came together, the inevitable result would be the absorption of the Red by the Mississippi, and a rush of most of its waters down the stream of the greatest slope and velocity.

This becomes the more evident when we reflect that the Red debouched directly into the Mississippi, and that it was furthermore completely cut-off from its natural outlet—the Atchafalaya.

As the Mississippi, at that time, swept entirely around the bend now called Old River, and as the Atchafalaya became rafted in the manner before shown, the Red River would continue to flow into it as a forced tributary, until some subsequent great change should divert its course and direct it elsewhere.

Throughout all the delta of the Mississippi, it is well known that its banks fall rapidly back from the river latterally, and consequntly the parallel back valley must be on a lower level on the same parallel of latitude. Hence the Red River, running through this lower valley, must necessarily be below the Mississippi; and this being universal on every parallel, it is evident that the plane of its slope has a less inclination also. In consequence, during its floods, and even at low water, the Mississippi would back up its waters into the former; and as these back waters had no natural outlet, they would be forced up the Red, Black, Ouachita and Little Rivers, and their numerous branches, perhaps for many miles. This would produce a constant retardation of the current of lower Red River, and a consequent precipitation of the earthy matter held in suspension, as this latter is lifted and carried along entirely by the velocity of the current, or by the mechanical action of the water in motion, as we have before seen. These depositions would cause the lower part of its channel to shoal; and the waters coming down from above together with the back waters from the Mississippi, finding no sufficient vent, would escape in a sheet, flow over the banks into the low bordering swamps, thus converting nearly all of this entire region into one vast reservoir, as far as the retardation extended.

No great and sudden changes can ever be made in an alluvial stream, however, without producing great efforts on the part of nature to restore herself to her primary condition, or its equivalent. Hence the natural efforts of the back water in the Red River basin would have been directed towards cutting a new channel around and to the west of the Atchafalaya, in order to take the lower level of its valley to the sea.

The physical difficulties, however, attending the making of a new channel are well known. A cut-off, artificially made, and having all the advantages of a fall of from ten to twenty times greater than that of the stream in which it is made, is nevertheless many years in cutting an equal section, and crevasses upon the Mississippi, which are a type of the manner in which nature would have worked in the case in question, frequently pass away without leaving any permanent excavated traces of their existence. Indeed, they plough furrows, and the corn and cane stubble remain in many cases as if the disturbing cause had been nothing more violent than a heavy flooding rain.

It is plain, therefore, that the back waters in Red River could not have excavated a new channel for themselves, but could only have escaped laterally in a sheetflow over the lower levels of the valley of the Atchafalaya, to its entire submersion in times of floods.

This is obvious from the fact that the water once discharged into this lower valley could never return again to the Mississippi by the same channel. Consequently the meeting had forced the Red River to be tributary to the Mississippi, and its valleys to become a reservoir for the discharge of the surplus floods of the latter, partially on account of the rafting of the Atchafalaya.

EFFECTS UPON THE MISSISSIPPI.

The sudden accession of the waters of Red River to its volume would cause the Mississippi to change its regimen. This change could not have been very great or sudden, however, as the Atchafalaya, until it became rafted, partially compensated for the accession from Red River. In time this river accommodated itself to the new order of things, discharging its surplus in the meanwhile over both of its banks into the low swamps behind.

It is plain, furthermore, that at that time there could have been no question of low water navigation, excepting at the mouth of and in Lower Red River, as what is Old River now was then the Mississippi.

Such had probably been the condition of these rivers for ages, and this was their condition and their several relations at the time they were first discovered by the Europeans, and thence up to the year 1831, when our troubles regarding navigation began to be really serious.

SHREVE'S CUT-OFF.

It is irrelevant to this discussion to introduce the changes wrought by civilization in the establishment of its homesteads, and in preparing the lands for cultivation. Nor yet is it effected, up to this point, by the commencement of levees in and around the city of New Orleans in 1727, and their gradual extension up and down the coast, until, as at present, the Mississippi is confined within parallel embankments. These had nothing whatever to do with our present difficulties in the low water navigation between the Red and the Mississippi rivers.

The causes of their origin were very different; and it only adds another instance to the long list of evils which have resulted from the many partial works constructed in this State, entered into without due survey and reflection, and executed without intelligence or skill, for the doubtful benefit of one section of the State, to the prejudice and injury of many others. What was here attempted as an amelioration of a partial evil, was largely productive of a greater, as, indeed, might have been ascertained upon due investigation. I allude to the cut-off made by Captain Shreve, in 1831. To improve the navigation out the mouth of and in Lower Red River, which was rapidly deteriorating, from the deposition at its mouth, caused by checking the current, as we have before seen, recourse was had to this popular but pernicious method of obtaining immediate relief.

A perfect cut-off produces, together with other results, a sudden fall of the whole river at and above the point where made.

It is hence evident that there would result temporarily, from this work, the immediate benefit required. The Mississippi having suddenly fallen at the mouth of Red river, there would necessarily be less back water in the latter, and consequently an increased current and greater fall.

Red River would, therefore, tend to free itself from the shoal bars at its mouth, and to wash out the light deposits which had accumulated in its bed for some distance above. This benefit could not of necessity be permanent or lasting. For, by thus throwing the Mississippi further to the east, it was partially separated from Red River, and, to a certain degree, both rivers were forced to assume their original independent channels.

Several natural causes would tend to widen, if not to complete, this separation, two of which, especially, were prominently active:

First—The tendency of the Mississippi to close up the gorges of its old bend by annual deposits in them. This is an invariable law, which operates in every cut-off, whether natural or artificial; and of the effects of which lakes St. John and Concordia, in the parish of Concordia, a short distance above, may be instanced as perfect specimens on the Mississippi. There are many other similar cut-offs throughout the State, which have completely closed their gorges by this same process, and which are familiar to every one.

Second—The renewed efforts of the Red River to reach the Gulf by the lower levels of the Atchafalaya, from the increased activity which it received under this change of regimen and artificial separation. Additional power and increased activity were also given to the operations of these natural causes by the labors of man. For, in 1833, two years after the cut-off had been made, a Board of Public Works was incorporated, under which the internal improvements of the State began to be developed. The removal of the rafts obstructing the Atchafalaya and Grand Rivers and Bayou Sorrel, being urgently demanded by the necessities of the case, was among the earliest of its operations. In order to open the navigation through these streams to the Attakapas, a labor required by an increasing population, man performed by the removal of these rafts that which nature was unable to do without such assistance, as we have before seen.

When these rafts were partially broken and removed, the increased current velocity of the Atchafalaya soon washed out the light deposits in its channel. By the annual assistance which it received from the Internal Improvement Department, this river rapidly assumed its original capacity to vent the waters of Red River, with an increased ability to carry off the back waters discharged into the Red River basin by the Mississippi. The efforts of both of the latter rivers were joined in the same direction — the Red River striving to regain its natural outlet by the lower levels of this valley, supplied water and current for the abrasion, and the Mississippi, by using the lower Red and all of Old River as a reservoir, greatly weakened and retarded the currents in the latter, and hence there resulted a rapid precipitation of alluvial deposit and consequent shoaling throughout the entire channel of Old River. Its lower gorge was closed in a few years, while bars and shoals were more gradually forming in the upper gorge, and islands and shoals in all that part of its channel from the mouth of the Red River to the Mississippi. Besides, the Mississippi kept receding further to the east by a vigorous abrasion of its left bank, while as rapidly batturing the right bank and filling the gorges of its old bend, until it has taken up an equated position at some considerable distance from the place where Shreve originally cut his channel.

It is plain from these facts that this cut-off, together with the removal of the Atchafalaya rafts, had in a great measure restored the Red and Mississippi rivers to their primary condition before the meeting of their waters, giving each a tendency to the Gulf by its own independent channel. The connection of the Red and Atchafalaya with the Mississippi was made to depend entirely upon the navigation of the old bend of the latter, now called Old River. This was rapidly filling up from the effects of natural causes. In short, the cut-off had only transferred the difficulty from the mouth of the Red to the channel of Old River, and had greatly impaired the navigation, instead of improving it.

In its annual report for January, 1839, the old Board of Public Works reports as follows :

"Since the meeting of the Board, in May last, we have learned that the effects of the cut-off in the Mississippi, near Red River, has produced considerable obstruction to the navigation of the latter stream, and that fears were entertained that the communication with the Mississippi would be lost."

This was before the rafts were entirely removed from the Atchafalaya, as P. O. Hebert, State Engineer, reports in 1847, that this river "was filled with raft and floating drift, from two miles above Bayou Pigeon to within seven miles of its head," which obstructions were not removed completely until within the past few years.

Thus, from the time the Shreve cut-off was made, in 1831, up to the year 1839, and for every subsequent year thereafter, the navigation of Old River deteriorated more and more, until it became the subject of universal complaint to all of the sections of the State at all interested in having it kept open.

RACCOURCI CUT-OFF.

Among the many plans suggesting themselves for the amelioration of the low-water navigation of Old River, it is singular that no other method could be thought of than the recurrence to a second cut-off, especially after the experience of the fatal consequences of the first. With this object in view, however, the Raccourci cut-off was proposed and finally completed in 1847.

Here is another instance of hasty legislation rushing into unknown and greater evils, merely to escape for the moment an existing one. Notwithstanding the efforts made by P. O. Hebert, State engineer, to arrest the progress and final execution of this work—and in despite of the warnings of other engineers of scientific attainments, who cautioned the Legislature that this proposed cut-off would not produce the benefits expected of it, but that it would only cause the inundation of lower Louisiana—still, this last crowning work was ordered into execution.

As was predicted of it, and as might have been anticipated from the character of its effects, this work led to an early and complete separation of the Red and the Mississippi Rivers, by giving additional power and activity to all the causes which we have seen in operation, assisting them the more rapidly to destroy this very navigation through Old River, which it had been made to improve.

This cut-off was completed in 1847. Since then Old River has filled up, not gradually, but with extraordinary rapidity. Every river pilot will confirm this; and it is, furthermore, attested by the annual legislation in vogue by general complaint for its improvement. Since that time, furthermore, the rafts in the Atchafalaya have been completely broken, and to a great extent removed, so that its channel is now widened and deepened to something like its original capacity and magnitude.

The rapidity of the changes resulting to Old River from these cut-offs is fully illustrated by the following attached lithographic maps:

Map A.—From the map of M. Bm. Lafon, civil engineer, made in 1805, which shows the relations between the Mississippi, Red and Atchafalaya Rivers, twenty-six years before Shreve's cut-off was made.

Map B.—From the surveys and maps of George T. Dunbar, Engineer Board of Public Works, made in 1839, eight years after the cut-off was made, which faithfully illustrates the filling of the gorges of its old bend by the Mississippi. It also exhibits the soundings in these gorges at the time, as well as those at the mouth of Red River and at the head of the Atchafalaya.

Map C.—From the surveys and soundings of L. Hebert, State engineer, made in 1855 and in 1856, showing the further progress of the filling of the gorges, and the formation of islands in the upper part of the Loop cut-off, from the mouth of Red River to the Mississippi.

This map was made after the rafts were removed from the Atchafalaya. A comparison of the soundings laid down upon this map with those upon Dunbar's map, made fifteen years before, shows the rapidity of the deepening of the head of the Atchafalaya after the removal of its rafts and the increased velocity of its current.

Maps D and E, on file in this office, exhibit still further changes, subsequent to the making of the Raccourci cut-off, and its effects upon the gorges of its old bend.*

In consequence, therefore, of the making of these cut-offs and the removal of the Atchafalaya rafts, nature has at length triumphed in the execution of her universal and unchangeable laws. And while the Legislatures of 1859 and 1860 were passing the foregoing acts, anticipatory of a separation of the Red and Mississippi rivers, that

---

*These maps alluded to were destroyed at Baton Rouge, but were similar to those herewith.

result had in reality already taken place, for all the practical purposes of low water navigation, and the waters of the Red and the
Atchafalaya were effectually blended into one stream, flowing majes-
tically in one unbroken channel of over two thousand miles, from
the Rocky Mountains to the Gulf of Mexico.

This has probably been the case for several years past; and it
will be endeavored to be proven, further on in this report, that this
separation has been anything but a misfortune to the best interests
of the State.

PROOFS OF THE DESTRUCTION OF NAVIGATION.

In evidence of the complete destruction of the low water navigation, I will adduce the following facts :

In July last, between the first and nineteenth of the month, when
there was about five feet of water over the bar at the mouth of Old
River, the surface currents invariably set in, in every instance, from
the Mississippi towards the mouth of Red River, and with the following velocities:

At two miles from the mouth the current was at that time 1.7 feet
per second, at two and three-quarter miles it was 1.3 feet per second,
below the islands in the channel of Old River the current was 1.0
feet, still setting in. Continuing in the same direction, the right
hand channel around the islands had a current of 0.66 feet per
second, and the left hand channel a current of 1.2 feet per second,
both setting in.

The surface current of Red River set up stream from its mouth at
the rate of 0.45 feet per second, whence it slacked up to a point
above five miles above the mouth, and then came to a stand or dead
water.

The current through the head of the Atchafalaya was at the same
time 4.16 feet per second.   At the distance of one mile from the head
its current was 2.1 feet per second, and three miles below it was
2.0 feet, which is about its average velocity there for that stage of
water.

The mean areas of the water sections of the mouths of these three
rivers were at the same time as follows :

Old River .... 9,119 square feet.
Red River .... 30,741 square feet.
Atchafalaya .... 7,061 square feet.

These selectional areas and velocities give us the following discharging capacities :

Atchafalaya...................... 29,390 cubic feet per second.
Red River .... 13,833 cubic feet per second.
Old River...................... 19,149 cubic feet per second.

In other words, the discharge of the Atchafalaya, at that time, exceeded the combined discharge of both the Red and Old Rivers—as the back current in the Red River more than compensates for the slight excess. It is plain, therefore, that the Atchafalaya discharged not only the waters of Red River, but also those of Old River, which are wholly supplied from the Mississippi. The back water in Red River retarding its current, makes it equally evident that a constant deposition is going on at its mouth, and in the lower part of its course. There are disturbing causes around the mouth of Old River which form eddies, which frequently give its current the appearance of running out into the Mississippi. This has led casual observers to suppose that the currents of Old River are variable, and that they sometimes set in and sometimes set out at the same stage, in proportion as the supply from the Mississippi or from the Red River prevails. This is not the fact, however, and it is clearly disproved by testing the current at any point beyond the influences mentioned, when it will be found that the Mississippi invariably sets into Old River at all stages of water. This is so obvious from the fact of the lower levels of the valley of Red River that it would hardly seem to require proof.[*]

Character of the Bar.—The great difficulties in the navigation of Old River during low water arise principally from the bar at its immediate mouth and the many increasing shoals around and below the islands in the wider part of the channel. These latter shoals are getting worse and more numerous every year. The bar at the mouth is composed of very light and shifting alluvial deposit, which is constantly changing its position under the influences of the current, but more especially under that of the eddies already mentioned.

In July last, these changes were so rapid that a boat, in passing over the bar on her up trip, was almost sure to run aground in taking the same channel on her return. The Anna Perret, drawing five feet, grounded in going up on the nineteenth of July, by attempting

---

[*]Mr. Duncan is here mistaken; in August, 1873, we gauged the river, and found a good current flowing out of each mouth of Old River.—M. J. S.

the same channel which she had safely taken a few days before in coming down. After lying there some twelve hours, the soundings on her port side gave only one foot in depth from stem to stern, the light sands constituting the bar having drifted around her to that depth in this short space of time.

On the twelfth of August the mouth was entirely closed to the passage of the Catahoula, at which time there was from eighteen to twenty inches of water upon the bar. It was subsequently reported to have fallen still lower.

On the twenty-eighth of September, shortly after one of the small class steamboats had ploughed her way through the bar, there was obtained, by accurate measurements, the following results:

Actual width of water channel........ .... 170 feet.
Average depth of channel .... 2.959 feet.
Sectional water area (about)...................... 503 sq.feet.

Upon a due examination of the foregoing facts, the following conclusions are apparent to every one:

I. That the low water navigation of Old River is completely destroyed for all practical purposes; and that as the same causes are still operating, it must necessarily deteriorate more and more every year.

II. That the water supply of Old River is due to the Mississippi, both at high and low stages, and not to the Red River.

III. That the Red and Atchafalaya rivers are unquestionably one and the same stream now, whatever may have been their former relations.

IV. And that there is a constant deposit at the mouth, and in lower Red River, owing to the retardation of its current by the back waters of the Mississippi.

Hence, Old River now can only be regarded as a communication between the Red, Atchafalaya, and the Mississippi during the continuance of high waters, at which time it also acts as a water-waste to the surplus floods of the latter.

PLANS OF IMPROVEMENT PROPOSED.

The question then arises, what can be done to improve the low-water navigation of Old River? We are now in a position to profitably introduce into this discussion the several projects proposed by the Legislature in the foregoing acts. We will take them up in their chronological order. Act No. 269 of 1859, calls for the preservation of the navigation of Old River, and the prevention of the impending separation between the Red and Mississippi Rivers.

Now we have seen that the navigation of the former has already been destroyed, and that the separation of the latter has already been effected, for all practical purposes, as far as low-water navigation is concerned, which is obviously the sense of the act. The question then changes and becomes, how can we restore this low-water navigation in the one case, and thus renew the connection of these rivers in the other? Can these results be obtained by completely damming Old River below the mouth of the Red, in order to cut off the Atchafalaya from its source of supplies, as proposed in act No. 29 of 1860; or will a partial closing of the head of the Atchafalaya be productive of the object desired, as proposed in act No. 30 of 1860?

Let us answer these in their order.

DAM ACROSS OLD RIVER.

It is wholly practicable to construct such a dam as is here proposed, which will forever dissolve the present connection between the Red and Atchafalaya Rivers, and which will force the Red River to become the tributary of the Mississippi, so that we will secure the permanent low water navigation desired. To accomplish this, however, it is evident that wing levees must be extended to connect with the Mississippi levees from one end of the dam, and to connect with the levees on Red River from the other. Otherwise there would be a lateral escape of the waters of Red River flowing behind and around the dam, in their efforts to regain the lower levels of the Atchafalaya. In thus making the Red River a tributary of the Mississippi, advantage should be taken of the superior capabilities of the lower branch of Old River for the purpose. This we can accomplish by throwing our dam directly across the head of the Atchafalaya, and by cutting a canal through the narrow neck of batture, between the upper and lower branches of Old River, to establish the connection at that point.

The reasons for this are: That this lower branch was the original slope of the Mississippi; that it has a more natural and less abrupt curve for the discharge of the water; because it is deeper and is not obstructed with islands and shoals, and because it has a greater descent in its water plane.

Although I consider this work practicable, and capable of accomplishing the ends in view, yet, nevertheless, I am forced to abandon it for other reasons. Its cost will be immense, yet not so great as to render its feasibility nugatory, were it not for the evil consequences which its adoption will produce, which are provided against in the act, and which will be discussed in this report hereafter.

ESTIMATED COST OF THIS PLAN.

	Cubic Yards.
Dam across the head of the Atchafalaya.	195,600
Levees to connect the ends of the dam with the levees on the Red and the Mississippi rivers at the nearest points*.	3,691,306
Cutting canal through batture, between the upper and lower branches of Old river†.	75,777
Total cubic yards of cutting and embankment. .	3,962,683
Which, at twenty-five cents per cubic yard, will cost.	$990,670 75
Add for contingencies, inspections, etc.	5,329 25
Total cost.	$996,000 00

The necessary expenses of increasing the height of the levees on the Mississippi, on both banks, above and below the mouth of Old River, are not included in the above estimates.

PARTIALLY CLOSING THE HEAD OF THE ATCHAFALAYA.

Relative to this project, its feasibility is increased by using the lower branch of Old River, and by cutting a canal to connect with the upper branch, for the reasons before given. The only proper and effectual manner of constructing this work is to carefully groine the left bank of the head of the Atchafalaya to prevent its further abrasion. Then to construct a powerful breakwater from the other bank, with protecting groined wings, and to project nearly across the head of the stream.

Furthermore, such a curve and direction must be given to the breakwater to direct the current of Red River through the lower branch of Old River, and thence through the canal to the upper branch.

By this method of constructing the work we have surrounded it

---

* This great cost would be saved if the dam is placed at Simmsport, as the levees have been constructed.—M. J. T.

† This canal has been cut by the river itself, and is now open.—M. J. T.

with every favorable circumstance. We have substituted the deep water of lower Old River for the shoal and difficult navigation of its upper branch and have reduced the difficulties of the problem to the bar at the immediate mouth of Old River, and a shoal channel of only two miles in length from the canal *a. b.* to the mouth.

As we have partly closed its natural outlet, a larger volume of Red River would necessarily be thrown through this new channel, and to some extent, upon the shifting bar at the mouth of Old River. When the differences of level between the Red River and the Mississippi are considered, it is not safe to presume that this increase of water will have any great scouring velocity, which alone would make it successful.

On the contrary, it is evident that our breakwater only acts as a partial dam, and by making a reservoir of Old River, some water is per force discharged into the Mississippi from a certain rise in the reservoir, nothing more. It is evident, therefore, that we will still have to dredge the bar annually in order to secure our low water navigation, and by harrowing and scraping throughout the reduced distance during low stages, we would probably preserve this communication for a few years to come.

ESTIMATED COST OF THIS WORK.

Cutting canal through batture between upper and lower Old River, 75,777 cubic yards.

Which at 25 cents per cubic yard will cost............$18,944 25
Break water with groined wings complete.............. 35,000 00
Contigencies, inspections, etc. 2,055 75

Total cost......................................'............$56,000 00

There will be an annual expenditure in harrowing and scraping, not included in the above estimate.

Of the two plans under consideration, this is unquestionably the least objectionable in its consequences. The first would be permanent, however, whereas the last could only delay the evil day for a few years, within which time the natural causes at work would bring us back exactly to our present condition. A large sum of money would have been expended thus to secure a temporary benefit; as nothing is hazzarded in predicting the ultimate failure of this method, arising from the same causes which now produce the bars,

4

shoals and islands in Old River. To accomplish the ends in view, and solve the problem thoroughly, the works constructed must be permanently successful. Otherwise there would be a constant expenditure of money for useless and impracticable results.

Plan proposed by L. Hebert, State Engineer. The second section of act No. 262, of 1859, requires the recommendations made by L. Hebert, State Engineer, in his special report of February 7, 1859, on Bayou Cut-Off, to be taken as the basis of the future surveys for the improvements under discussion; and as these surveys were completed under the direction of that officer, and a project predicated upon them, it will be proper in this connection to examine the works which have been proposed by that gentleman.

His plan to improve the navigation through Old River, and to preserve the connection between the Red and the Mississippi rivers, as given in his special report of March, 1860, is as follows: To gradually close the Atchafalaya, at Simmsport, with a dam, with wing levees extending from the one end of this dam up the left bank of the Atchafalaya to Old River, and thence around to connect with the Mississippi levees.

From the other, or western terminus of the dam, the levees are to extend along the lower (right) bank of Bayou Des Glaize, from Simmsport to Moreauville, where the Des Glaize is to be diked; thence to the Avoyelles prairies at the nearest point, and from the other side of these prairies across to the Red River, below Bayou Chanctaw, and finally up the Red River to connect with its levees below Alexandria on the right bank.

It is furthermore proposed to open the Latanache as an outlet, to compensate for the water thrown into the Mississippi by the Red River, and as a source of supply for the Atchafalaya. In connection, also, to raise and strengthen the levees on both sides of the Mississippi, for fifty miles above the mouth of Old River down to its mouth.

It is obvious that this plan forces the Red to become tributary to the Mississippi, and that in its general features it satisfies the requirements of joint resolution No. 29, of 1860. It has another feature, however, wherein the resemblance ceases, and which must be discussed separately. This is the proposal to feed the Atchafalaya from the Mississippi through the Latanache, converting this latter, at the same time, into an outlet for the relief of the Mississippi.

Now the Latanache heads in the bend of the Old River, resulting from the Raccourci cut-off. The upper gorge of this bend has already been closed completely by natural causes, fulfilling the constant law of all cut-offs, as we have previously seen. In a like manner, also, the lower gorge has greatly filled up, so that at the present. time it is obstructed by a bar. which completely closes it to cause navigation in low water. The difficulties attending the making of a new channel, or enlarging an old one, even under the most favorable circumstances, are well known; and hence it is reasonable to conclude, from the many obstacles surrounding the present case, that a century may perhaps elapse before the Latanache will enlarge sufficiently to equal the present discharge of the Atchafalaya, if, indeed, it ever enlarges at all under the circumstances. Therefore, we may safely throw this element out of the future discussion.

ESTIMATED COST OF THIS PLAN.

	Cubic yards.
Dam across the Atchafalaya at Simmsport (taken same as at bend)...............................	195,600
Wing levees to connect with the levees of Red River and the Mississippi	3,691,306
Dam across Des Glaize at Moreauville............	13,333
Opening Latanache and straightening same........	2,640,000
Leveeing both banks of the Latanache, from the Mississippi to Atchafalaya......................	1,689,600
Total cubic yards.............	8,229,839
Which, at twenty-five cents per cubic yard of excavation and embankment will cost................	$2,057,459 75
Add for contingencies, inspections, etc	6,540 25
Total cost of plan......................	$2,064,000 00

The cost of raising and strengthening the levees on the Mississippi as proposed is not included in the foregoing estimate.

A work is impracticable to a State as to an individual, when it is beyond the means of the one or the other; and perhaps the expenditure of over two millions of dollars upon a single State work, even of the great importance and general character of this, is beyond the present means of the State of Louisiana.

My objection to this method of attaining the objects in view are not founded upon its cost, however, but upon other considerations much more serious in their character and consequences, as I shall now proceed to show :

INUNDATION RESULTING FROM THE ADOPTION OF EITHER OF THE PROPOSED PLANS.

Another element of the very highest importance here enters into the discussion of this question: This is the effects which will be produced by inundation upon the adjacent and distant country, and the changes of regimen, slope and velocity, which will be assumed by these several rivers and their tributaries, resulting in time of flood from the adoption of either of these proposed works. This will be simplified by showing the present condition and relations of these several rivers and their adjacent tributaries, when the changes resulting from either plan will become the more apparent.

Present Relations.—As things now exist, we have the Red and the Atchafalaya rivers constituting one and the same stream, which flows in a valley nearly parallel with that of the Mississippi, and connected with the latter during high water by that waste river called Old River.

Owing to the rapid lateral slope of the banks of the Mississippi everywhere, this parallel back valley, occupied by the Red and the Atchafalaya, must be below that of the former river, and consequently their high and low water marks must necessarily be below the high and low water marks of the Mississippi for the corresponding stage on the same parallel of latitude. These facts are demonstrated by the lines of levels run on every parallel, which we will illustrate by the following examples:

First—The section through Bayou Cut-off, made in November, 1857, gives the following water levels: High water mark of Red River three feet below that of the Mississippi. Low water mark of Red River five feet below the low water mark of the Mississippi.

Second—A line run between the two rivers, about two miles south of Bayou Cut-off, gives the high water mark of Red River three and eight-tenths feet below that of the Mississippi.

Third—The high water mark of the Atchafalaya is fourteen and one-tenth feet below that of the Mississippi, through the Latanache section.

Fourth—The high water mark at Indian Village is twenty and two-tenths feet below that of the Mississippi.

Fifth—There is no difference in the levels of the high water marks of the Mississippi at Towas' and that of the mouth of Red River, owing to their direct connection through Old River.

Sixth—The high water mark at the head of the Atchafalaya is seven-hundredths feet below that of the Mississippi at Towas', showing that these differences of level hold good, even through the Old River section; and similar results would be shown by the sections or any other parallel.

From Bayou Cut-off to the mouth of the Old river, a distance of twenty-one miles by way of the Mississippi, the fall of the latter is 7.87 feet, or nearly 4.5 inches per mile. The distance from the same bayou, by way of the Red River to the mouth of the latter, is about fifteen miles, and the fall of the Red River between these points is 2.72 feet, or a little over two inches to the mile. Hence we have lower levels and a less inclination of the plane of descent of the Red River, compared with that of the Mississippi.

It is conclusive, therefore, that the waters of the Mississippi must flow into the Red and the Atchafalaya rivers, even at the lowest stages, as its water marks are higher at every stage. This fact has already been indicated in the currents through Old River previously given.

It is equally conclusive, furthermore, that the Mississippi, during high water, will back up the Red River, owing to the lesser inclination of its slope, directly in proportion to the height of the water mark in the Mississippi above that of the Red River. Therefore, it requires no further demonstration to prove that the only possible case in which any of the waters of the Red River could flow into the Mississippi, through Old River, would be when the former should rise, from some extraordinary cause, above the water marks of the Mississippi upon the same parallel of latitude. Such cases must naturally be so rare and unusual as to justify us in throwing its consideration out of the question. Hence we have now two injurious effects to Red River and its adjacent country from the Mississippi waters through Old River:

First—The deterioration and complete destruction of the low water navigation of Old River, ruining the trade and commerce of Red River and the Attakapas.

Second—The retardation of the Red River current at and above its mouth, and the consequent shoaling of that part of its channel, causing, besides, a gentle overflow of the surrounding low country during low water.

During the prevalence of high water or floods, the question assumes a very different aspect. The Mississippi then rushes through the gorges of Old River, and finding the high water slope of the Red River of easier descent than its own, and the Atchafalaya being unable to vent these additional waters as rapidly as they are forced upon it, they are necessarily backed up the Red River for many miles, overflowing its banks and flooding the entire country.

Every ordinary high water backs up as far as the falls at Alexandria; and at times of extreme floods, the waters are backed even above the falls. They are well known to extend up the Black River, and thence up the Ouachita to the mouth of Bayou Bartholemew, a a distance of over three hundred miles.

This back water also extends up the Tensas and Little rivers, as well as through all the outlets and branches of these several streams, overflowing all of the adjacent low country.

The current of the back water is sometimes so great at Trinity, the junction of the Ouachita, Tensas and Little rivers, that it has been known in its first rise to transport rafts up the Ouachita to Harrisonburg, from that point.

REPORT OF COMMISSION OF ENGINEERS FOR 1872.

In the year 1850, Professor Forshey wrote his report of the Atchafalaya survey under Senator Ricker. General Thompson aiding, we have repeated these soundings in July, 1872, finding no material difference in either the depth or width of the Atchafalaya in the twenty-two years past. The mean width about 730 feet and the mean high-water depth at source about fifty fee : mark of 1850. High-water mark here of 1850 about two feet below 1828. We found, moreover, that at a stage of water nineteen feet below highest mark, at source of Atchafalaya, with no special freshet in either of the rivers related to the movements here, the Red River was pouring only one-third her waters into the Atchafalaya and two-thirds into the Mississippi. For example, we measured the cross section and velocity of Red River, half a mile above the mouth in Old River, and found it discharging 93,730 cubic feet per second. We measured the Atchafalaya just below Coville Bayou, an inlet two miles down, and found 35,584 cubic feet. The difference, 58,156 cubic feet, should be found passing out of Red River into the Mississippi.

We then measured Red River, below Old River, in its channel toward the Mississippi, and found 56,941 cubic feet passing into the great river.

We thus verified our measurements with satisfactory approximation.

The disposition found at the natural mouth of Red River to shoal up during low water and render navigation difficult does not now bring the apprehensions of former days. Every high water cuts out the channel again and restores about the same soundings as for many years past.

One striking feature has been manifested the past summer. After the recession of the summer high water, it was found that a channel had cut through the lower channel of Old River, entirely closed and covered with forests for more than twenty years. The survey of 1850 notes the complete closure of this lower mouth. The trees are caving in and the channel of navigation is now through that channel.

The distance to the gulf from the source of the Atchafalaya by way of Grand Lake and Berwick's Bay is only one hundred and five miles. The distance by the Mississippi is three hundred and twenty-six miles, or about three times the distance.

That portion of Red River which reaches the Gulf by the Mississippi route, fall the fifty feet to the sea at 1.84 inches per mile. That which runs down the Atchafalaya, falls the same amount at the rate of 5.7 inches per mile. Yet this is not the strongest river. The Atchafalaya accomplishes more than forty-two feet of its fall in the first seventy miles to Grand and other lakes. This will give nearly eight inches per mile. Besides that, the channel is free from the great tortuousness that marks the Mississippi's channel. Hence, all things considered, the tendency of this river to ravage its banks is extreme.

We had, therefore, expected much greater changes in depth and width than we found. Neither has occurred to an extent to verify the apprehensions of the past. And though we will watch with the utmost vigilance the future behavior of the Atchafalaya, we would encourage the steamboat and navigation interest of Red River with the expectation that Red River will long maintain its present debouchure, and that the Atchafalaya will never again experience so disastrous a flood as in 1850, and before levees were built. The reasons are obvious. In the condition of the alluvion, before 1828, the absence of levees around the entire river front, from the Atchafalaya to some miles below the Red River landing, gave a free sweep to the floods, then two feet higher than in 1850, and full four feet higher than the highest water of 1858; and those floods quadrupled the inlet of the Atchafalaya itself. The levees are now complete around this bank and down the Atchafalaya for twenty miles and more. This levee will be extended down continuously to the Muscle Bayou and perhaps below on the left bank, and the entire right bank down a mile or two below the railroad crossing, some forty miles from its head.

COMMISSION OF ENGINEERS REPORT FOR 1873.

ATCHAFALAYA.

The only additional outlet, and the only one it is probably impracticable to close, is the Atchafalaya river. We examined the capacity of this channel at the same point as last year, and found no material change. There is a gradual, but very slow, abrasion of the channel and banks near and in the source of this stream. Both banks and the bottom, probably, are reveted and tied together with cypress stumps and roots, and the material is extremely tenacious red clay.

The Old River has opened its lower or right hand mouth, after more than twenty years closure, and now the waters are discharged through both mouths, the right hand mouth being much the larger. However, at low water, and at present, say six feet above low water, the most water and the navigable channel is again restored to the upper mouth.

During high water, then, the main body of Red River is carried down past the mouth, or head of the Atchafalaya river, thus increasing the tendency of the water to escape through its channel. It will be necessary to watch with much vigilance this tendency and to measure the discharge annually. The very rapid fall of the surface of the Atchafalaya down to nearly the sea level, places this outlet in the category of the Lafourche, and gives us the prospect of having to raise the levees on this stream to very high elevations. But we will not, at present, discuss this prospect. We have prescribed but few works upon the Atchafalaya, none that are entirely new, but intended to replace those formerly in existence where the lands in cultivation are imperiled.

FALLS AT ALEXANDRIA.

In Dunbar's report of 1840, he says, in regard to the falls at Alexandria :

The next and greatest obstruction to the low water navigation is the falls at Alexandria. This obstruction consists in a fall of three feet at low water above Bayou Rapides with two rapids, one mile above having a fall of one foot (vide plan G.) The rock forming the bed of the river consists of an extremely soft and friable sand stone, slightly impregnated with marl.

The stone yields readily to the knife or any hard body and may be crusted by the finger.

By consulting (plan G.) the soundings marking the channels will be seen. About fourteen hundred feet above the lower falls, the channel divides—One (the main channel) running over to the eastern and the other keeping close to the western shore, in a choice as to which of the two channels should be cleared. I had to consider two things; first the comparative expense of the two, and second the beneficial results to be produced. If we cut the eastern passage, we take the one chosen by nature and in this instance the most proper.

If the western, we throw the whole force of the current against the banks upon which the town is built and might cause the destruction of a large portion of the town.

The expense is in favor of the eastern channel; and I shall accordingly make my estimate for it. The profile on plan G. shows the section of the bed of the river, with the bar or beds of rock which it will be necessary to remove. The estimates are made for a channel sixty feet wide with depths of six and eight feet.

To give a passage of this description with six feet water, we would have to remove at the lower falls seven thousand three hundred and fifteen cubic yards, and at the upper, seven thousand four hundred and forty-nine cubic yards, making in all fourteen thousand seven hundred and sixty-four cubic yards, the cost of which would be, inclusive of dams and all expenses, fifteen thousand dollars. To give a depth of eight feet water we would have to remove at the lower falls sixteen thousand seven hundred and one cubic yards, and at the upper, eleven thousand and four yards, making in all twenty seven thousand seven hundred and five yards, which would cost twenty-eight thousand dollars, showing a difference of thirteen thousand dollars in the cost of the two channels.

The position of the falls is such that we must cut at least six feet into the rock to give six feet of water; a less depth would give too much fall and current, and in fact a deficiency of water. The difference of cost between the two depths appear considerable but is trifling compared with the benefit which the deeper channel would confer.

The current will be less violent, the boats, not having their keels as near the bed of the river, will be enabled to pass through much easier, and the channel will not be effected by any abrasion of the sides of the canal. Taking these things into consideration, I certainly recommend the deep channel.

It is useless for me to speak of the trifling cost of this improvement when compared with the immense benefits to be derived from it. Many of the legislative body live above this obstruction, and probably know what inconvenience and occasional suffering it occasions; with them the matter rests.

In 1842, Dunbar says:

In obedience to your resolution adopted at your May session, I advertised for proposals to remove the obstructions in Red River, created by the rapids near Alexandria, some short time after which I received a letter from an individual in that neighborhood, proposing to do the work, immediately after which I repaired to that place for the purpose of making the contract; but upon arriving there I found the person who had made the proposition not in a condition, or disposed to do so, in such manner as I could approve; and after viewing these rapids, and getting the best advice I could in relation to their removal, I returned home, under the apprehension that I should not be able to make the contract as designed. But such has not been the fact. Within a few weeks past, Captain Vawter, a gentleman now engaged under a contract with the government of the United States for the removal of the raft on Red River, presented himself to me, and offered to complete this work at the rapids in accordance with the survey and plan of our engineers, for a sum rather below that which was appropriated by the Legislature for that purpose; with the condition, on his part, to require no payment until the whole work was finished, and then to receive the same by such installments as are provided for by the act of the Legislature. The terms proposed, and the character and qualifications of the undertaker, Captain Vawter, were so favorable as to induce me at once to promise the contract. I have delayed its final completion, however, for reasons which I deemed sufficient, and which, under all the circumstances, the interest of the State required.

I desired to submit this matter again to the consideration of the board and to the Legislature, and I was impelled to this course from a fear that when these obstructions were removed at the point where they now exist, new ones of a similar character would present themselves at a point higher up the river. Such is the opinion of many persons with whom I conversed on the subject, and who, I am inclined to think, have a good knowledge of the river. A fear that their opinion might be correct, and that the expenditure of this heavy sum, appropriated at a time when our State was so much embarrassed by its pecuniary responsibilities, might be made without a corresponding benefit, induced me to incur the responsibility of postponing the completion of the contract; and I was strengthened in the propriety of this course from the fact that no injury could result from this delay, for the reason that the work can only be done when the water in the Red River is low. I now submit this matter to the Legislature and yourselves for new instructions.

In 1852 A. D. Wooldridge says:

Red River should be thoroughly cleaned from snags, and all timber growing beneath the banks cut close to the ground and into short pieces from the foot of the raft to the Couchatta Chute. A canal or channel should be cut fifty feet wide through the falls at Alexandria and all the water thrown into said channel, by walls laid in cement upon the rocks, across the balance of the river. I am convinced were this done that the present amount of water passing over the falls would give from five to seven feet depth in this channel, without in the least lowering the water above. In fact, that we should have better water in this channel than we now have on the bars above and below. The bars in Red River can not be removed. They are composed of quicksand, with one or two exceptions, and are constantly shifting with every stage of water, and with every accidental change of the current. In many places the only practicable channel is obstructed by fallen timber or snags. Were all these removed at the lowest stage of water the navigation would be vastly improved, and perhaps never entirely suspended. Without a personal inspection no one can have even a remote idea of the immense number of snags which show themselves at an extreme low stage of water in this river. I do not hesitate to say that there are in many bends from two to five thousand. In Rock River bend above Grand Ecore, or in a snaggy bend in the Bon Dieu, for instance, there are hundreds of places nearly as bad, and until all these are improved, all these snags cut or removed, will the people of upper Red River have to submit to exhorbitant charges for freight and passage during the period of low water.

In 1853, in the report of George W. Morse, State Engineer, to the General Assembly, we find:

I have thought it quite unnecessary that I should make a survey of the falls near Alexandria, in accordance with act No. 80 of the last Legislature, as the work of removing the obstructions, I know, was going on under the superintendence of Colonel De Russy, the able engineer appointed by the commissioners. I presume that after the examination and surveys which he has made, he will be able to demonstrate the utility of the work now in progress.

A stream which already brings to market about 300,000 bales of cotton, while its resources are not half developed, one-half of which at least, pays one dollar extra on account of the obstruction, without counting the extra cost of transporting other articles, is worthy of the very best improvement which can be adopted.

I have wished to obtain from Messrs. Maillefort & Raslorff the use of their apparatus for blasting under water, and also their aid and advice in the use of it, for the purpose of removing the wrecks of several old boats in the channels of our streams, and also to try an experiment with powder upon some of the rafts and stumps; such, for instance, as the floating rafts, like those which form in Bayou Sorrel, and upon the stumps, which very much impair the navigation in the lakes of Attakapas. I do not see that I have any legal authority under which I can obtain the services of these gentlemen without the passage of a special act, which, I hope, will be done as early as possible. Their patent does not extend to the use of powder for the purposes proposed, but by long practice in its use, they have unquestionably gained information which it might be well for every one to have who wished to commence the use of it.

I am glad to say that these gentlemen have most cheerfully promised to comply with my wishes and to lend me every assistance which it will be in their power to give. I expect very soon to obtain from them an estimate of the cost for which some of the above-mentioned operations can be carried out, which will enable me to ask for a special appropriation for this purpose.

From what is known about the great work of improvement already carried out by Mr. Maillefort in Hell Gate, near New York, as well as from my own observations at the falls at Alexandria, where these gentlemen are now at work, I have no doubt but that Mr. Maillefort's mode of blasting will prove very useful in our waters, and that it will be to the interest of the State to secure the use of such a powerful agency in the frequently occurring removal of wrecks, rafts, etc., from our navigable streams and bayous.

In 1854 George W. Morse says: It is probably my duty as State Engineer to call the attention of your honorable body to the present situation of the falls in Red River at Alexandria, and to the generally bad condition of that stream. Commissioners were appointed and money appropriated for the removal of the falls by an act of the Legislature, approved March 11, 1852. In the summer of 1853, an attempt was made to blast them out by Messrs. Maillefort & Raslorff, of New York, which certainly did not improve the condition of the river, and last year nothing was done, notwithstanding an additional appropriation was made for that purpose. It is high time that a stream which now brings to market nearly one-eighth of the cotton crop of the United States, and which will be doubled in the next ten years, should be relieved of such an embarrassing impediment to its navigation. I have not yet seen any reason to change the views expressed in my first annual report in reference to the necessity of locks at this point, except as to their location. I have had good opportunity during the last summer to make examinations of the rock, and have such samples in my office as will show clearly its character, from which I judge that a crane properly arranged for dredging, and attached to one of our heaviest State boats, would without difficulty excavate the required channel through it. The rock at the falls, when wet, can be easily cut with an axe or a crowbar, and if the spoon attached to the crane should meet with any hard substance which it would be unable to remove, it could be dislodged with powder or a falling bar of iron.

My examination have convinced me that there is room enough on the north side in the bed of the river, between the hill and the low-water in which to place a lock, which I would propose to construct partly of the hardest portion of the rock, and the rest of cast iron, the gates of which to be high enough to hold the water two or three feet above low-water mark only, so that when the river was up they should be open and entirely covered. Such a lock would not be very expensive if the excavations could be made with a dredge-boat; particularly, as with her crane she would deposit the earth on the outside so as to form a kind of coffer-dam in the shallow water, into which a part of the basin might run. This impediment costs the State in advanced prices of freight, not less than $300,000 upon an average per year ; and less than one half of that sum would remove it. A lock here, and wing-dams in a few other places, and light draft boats could at any time navigate the river from its mouth to Shreveport. There is always plenty of water, and all that we require besides the lock is to confine it. The importance of the stream demands more energetic appliances of improvement. The low water of 1850 and 1554 should not discourage, but rather stimulate our exertions; for a judicious expenditure of a sufficient sum to construct twenty or thirty miles of railroad, would carry us through to Shreveport on three and a half feet water, at any time, without difficulty; and during our ordinary low water seasons, such as has been experienced at any time, except in the years 1850 and 1854, we could easily obtain four feet. Our State boat, the Gov. Hebert, went to Alexandria on the twenty-third of December, 1854, at the very time when the water was lower than ever before known, and we are sure that she draws three and a half feet. While the State is expending millions upon railroads, why should it not employ four or five hundred thousand dollars to properly improve the navigation of this great river, which must, even after the completion of the roads, continue to carry to market nine-tenths of the produce of its valley, even if left in its present condition.

There is little or no doubt that most of the monetery disasters which have lately occurred in New Orleans would have been prevented if the produce which is ordinarily brought down Red River could have been forwarded at such prices as the planters were willing, or even able to pay. The merchants of New Orleans of course understand this matter better than I do, but it does seem to me, if the vast amount of cotton alone, which has been retained in the valley of Red River, had been added in time to the receipts in New Orleans, that it would have made some difference in the money market. It would have enabled the country merchants and planters to have paid their debts in the city, and given the merchants there the means of meeting their engagements. No reflecting mind, can, for one moment, entertain the opinion, that anything like the one-hundreth part of the planting interest situated upon the winding banks of Red River could be benefited in the way of sending their produce to market by railroad. No road could follow the sinuosities of the stream ; and who would send by it, unless it passed very near to them.

We have been accustomed to work upon about five hundred miles of this stream with only one boat, and that only a part of the year, causing a yearly expenditure to the State of a sum not sufficient to construct one-fourth of a mile of railroad; and then we complain that the river is not in good condition, and that the price of freights is enormous in low water. We require the labor of two hundred men on its banks, removing the timber to prevent the formation of new snags, for the term of about twelve months; and then four good boats for two seasons, to remove the obstructions already in the stream, locks at Alexandria, and wing-dams in two or three other places; after which we could leave it without any more work for ten years, and the navigation would be constantly improving. No timber would be left to fall in, and by washing out in the bends it would change its channel off of the beds of logs which we could not remove in the present one.

In the present condition of the river, two sets of low water boats are required, one above and the other below the falls, and being obliged to run in conjunction they are often found to wait at the falls, one for the other, thus losing time and adding to their expenses. By this arrangement, to carry on the business of the river, the same man or set of men, is obliged to own two boats. Whereas, if navigation were opened over the falls, one boat would run through without the costs attendant upon waiting or re-shipping, and boats would be constructed expressly for the low water trade; so that our low water prices for freight on cotton would then easily come down to $2 per bale, or $2 50 at the very highest, with up freights in proportion. If there should be any re-shipment, it would occur at the mouth of Red River. Not that sufficient depth of water would not be found there, but because larger boats could be used on the Mississippi river. It may be thought that I am extravagant when I speak of an expenditure of four or five hundred thousand dollars, and probably the improvements would not cost near that sum; but when we speak of railroads we talk of millions with unshaken nerve.

From report of Louis Hebert, State Engineer, 1856:

* * * * * * *

Nothing has been done, I believe, during the year, upon the falls at Alexandria. In my annual report I strongly recommended the construction of locks upon one or the other falls. I must here repeat my recommendation. Nothing else will do; and the large commerce of Red River (large even now, and increasing so as to be at some day almost incalculable) warrants any outlay, even to millions of dollars.

* * * * * * *

He next takes into consideration the project of rendering the Rapides and Jean de Jean a canal of circumnavigation around the falls, and proves that four locks would be necessary in each stream, and estimates that each lock would cost no less than $35,000. The rise of Red River in 1849 being forty-one feet above the low water of 1856, the locks would not prevent the overflow of the Rapides country.

All of which is respectly submitted.

Most respectfully, your obedient servant,

M. JEFF THOMPSON,
Chief State Engineer.

Knowing that General B. B. Simms was well acquainted with the manner of removing the raft from the Atchafalaya, I addressed him a letter on the subject, and here give his reply:

NEW ORLEANS, January 12, 1874.

General M. Jeff. Thompson, Chief State Engineer, New Orleans, La:

DEAR SIR—In compliance with your request, I will briefly state: I have resided on the Atchafalaya from 1840 to 1870, during which period I have taken a lively interest in the general levee system of the State, having represented the parish of Pointe Coupee in both branches of the Legislature.

In reference to the Atchafalaya, the great obstructing raft in that stream was removed in the fall of 1839 (in the month of October) by fire. The raft had been for a number of years on the increase by the annual contributions of the Red, Ouachita, Black, and, last, though not least, the Mississippi rivers. I have seen the Atchafalaya so covered with drift that it would be with difficulty you could cross the river in a skiff.

Constant appeals to the State for aid without success induced a few of the citizens of the Atchafalaya, under the direction and lead of Captain Laird, to take the remedy in their own hands; and, availing ourselves of one of the seasons of greatest drought ever known in Louisiana, we went down in skiffs to the raft and set fire to the same. The result was that the fire swept over the raft, thirty miles in extent, destroying thousands of allegators and burning off the immense mass of timber thirty miles in length, and probably one hundred feet in heighth, to the water's edge. As soon thereafter as the water rose Captain Mayo, one of the most valuable officers of the State, was placed in charge of the State boats and found no difficulty in securing a passage through the raft for steamboats, and it has remained open to the present time.

In 1839 the water was so low at the mouth of the Atchafalaya that foot passengers, by means of a plank about fifteen feet long, could walk across it.

So soon as the raft was removed the river commenced widening and deepening, until it has seriously threatened to absorb the entire Red, Ouachita and Black Rivers. The old channel around by Turnbull's sugar house, in Old River, formerly the main channel, is almost entirely closed, and will, in a few years, form the solid land from the island to Concordia parish, and during the last low water the lower mouth was most seriously threatened. I am clearly of the opinion that unless some immediate action is had, and that without delay, that the Red River and its tributaries will seek the Gulf through the Atchafalaya, as that stream is constantly widening and deepening its bed, and it is fully capable of conducting off all the waters of those rivers.

I regret that I am unable to refer to the various reports on the subject, as my library was destroyed during the late unfortunate war.

In conclusion I take pleasure in stating that my views are fully in accord with our former State Engineer, General Hebert, who, I am happy to know, is a member of your board, and from whom you can derive much valuable information.

Asking you to excuse this hasty reply to your inquiries,

I am, General, very respectfully, your obedient servant,

B. B. SIMMS.

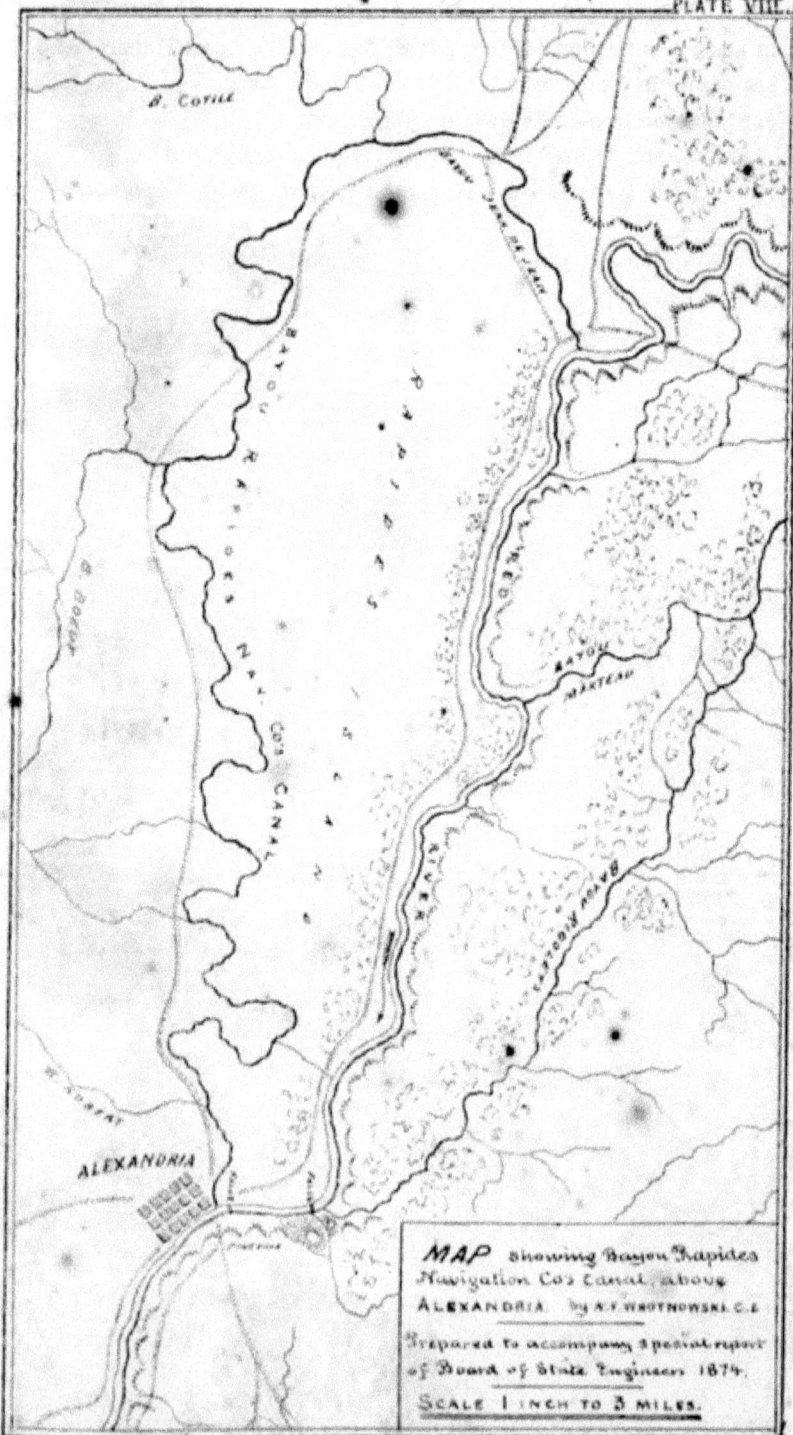

PLATE VIII

B. COTILE

BAYOU RAPIDES NAV. CO'S CANAL

ALEXANDRIA

MAP showing Bayou Rapides Navigation Co's Canal, above Alexandria. By A. F. Wrotnowski. C.E.

Prepared to accompany special report of Board of State Engineers 1874.

SCALE 1 INCH TO 3 MILES.

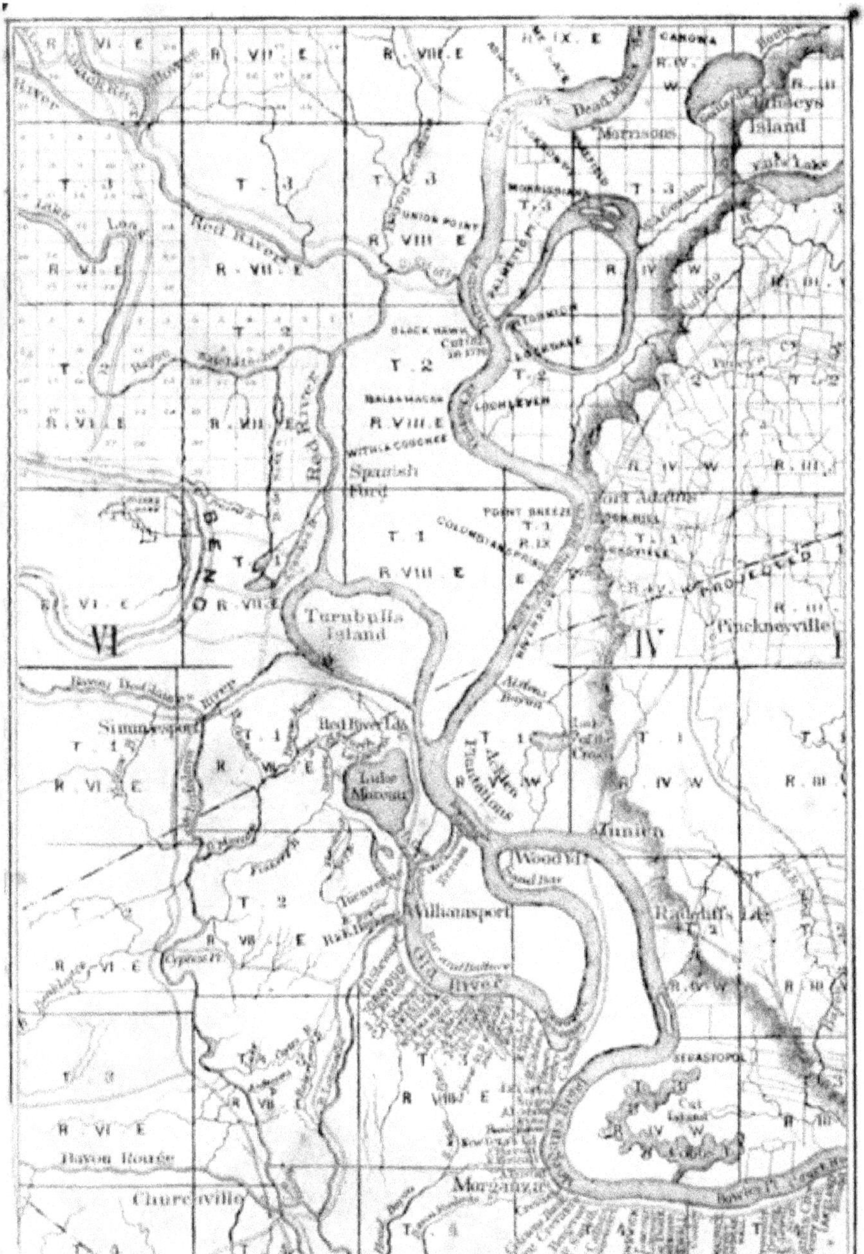
Red River
Turnbulls Island
Spanish Ford
Simmesport
Red River Ldg
Lake Moreau
Williamsport
Old River
Morganza
Churchville
Bayou Rouge
Cat Island
Tunica
Woodvil
Pinckneyville
Fort Adams
Morrisons
Radcliffs Lake
SEBASTOPOL
CANONA
BLACK HAWK
LOCH LEVEN
POINT BREEZE
UNION POINT
PALMETTO PT
MORRISSANIA
Acklen Plantations
Lake Concordia
Red River
Bayou